BURST

Topics for Today's Teens

Green Church

10 11 12 13 14 15 16 17 18 19 — 10 9 8 7 6 5 4 3 2 1

Editor: Josh Tinley
Design Manager: Keely Moore
Cover Design: Keely Moore

CONTENTS

INTRODUCTION

About Burst: Green Church

Why Green Church?

"Going green" is nothing new to teens today. They have grown up with recycling bins in their classrooms and annual Earth Day celebrations at school. Television channels such as Disney and Nickelodeon, which many youth watched as children and tweens, encourage viewers to "reduce, reuse, and recycle"; to conserve electricity by flipping the switch when leaving a room; and to turn off the water while brushing one's teeth. Many of their families have taken energy efficiency into account when purchasing new vehicles or appliances, whether to go green, to save some money, or both. Scouting organizations teach young people all sorts of eco-friendly habits while also giving them opportunities to experience firsthand the beauty of the natural world.

For American youth in the twenty-first century, the "three Rs" of conservation—reduce, reuse, and recycle—are as much a part of their education as the more traditional "three Rs"—reading, 'riting, and 'rithmatic. Christian teens do not need to be told to take shorter showers, to unplug phone chargers that aren't being used, or to find new uses for sour cream containers and ragged T-shirts. But they *do* need to understand how each action they take to heal or preserve the environment is an act of faith.

The biblical narrative begins with God creating the heavens and the earth and "all their multitude" (Genesis 2:1) and declaring all of creation "very good" (1:31). God gave humankind dominion over the earth and its creatures (1:28) and the responsibility to till and keep God's garden (2:15). The truths that the world in which we live is God's beloved creation and that God calls us to be caretakers of this creation are the basis of BURST: GREEN CHURCH. By caring for the earth, we are participating in God's work of healing a broken world. We are also showing love for our neighbors—present and future—by preserving and protecting the air, water, soil, and the other natural resources that are necessary for human survival and well-being.

Throughout this program, you and your youth will return to Scripture and reaffirm God's love of creation and humanity's role as stewards of the world in which we live.

4   Burst: Green Church

What Will Youth Learn From This?

The most important lesson that youth can learn from this study is that caring for the environment is an act of faith. Going green is not just something we do to make ourselves feel better or to be a part of the latest trend. For Christians, caring for the earth is a way to honor God and show our love for our neighbors. For this reason, BURST: GREEN CHURCH takes the usual "three *R*s" of conservation—*reduce, reuse,* and *recycle*—and adds three more—*reclaim, repent,* and *rejoice.* While it is important that Christians make responsible use of resources and avoid unnecessary waste and pollution, we also need to reclaim our role as caretakers of God's creation, repent of ways in which we have harmed or failed to care for creation, and rejoice in the glory of the heavens and earth that God crafted and declared "very good."

The hope of BURST: GREEN CHURCH is that the youth will come away from this study with:

- a greater appreciation of God's creation;

- a greater understanding of their role as stewards of God's creation;

- the understanding that caring for the world in which we live is an act of faith and a means of showing love for God and neighbor;

- several concrete ideas for ways that they can better preserve and protect God's creation by changing old habits and taking on new ones; and

- the encouragement to be leaders in their church and their community when it comes to being stewards of the environment.

How Do I Use This Resource?

This study is divided into six sessions:

- Session 1: Reclaim

- Session 2: Reduce

- Session 3: Reuse

- Session 4: Recycle

- Session 5: Repent

- Session 6: Rejoice

These sessions were designed with Sunday evening or mid-week youth fellowship in mind, but they could also work in the context of a Sunday school class or small-group Bible study. Each session begins with a three-page article for you, the leader. The purpose of these articles is to help you better understand each session's topic as it relates to Scripture and to youth today.

Each of these sessions also includes the following learning activities:

- **Open Your Eyes:** This introductory activity introduces each topic, often by inviting the youth to look at the subject in new ways.

- **Think It Through:** This activity introduces the youth to some of the issues facing God's creation.

- **Tune In:** This activity takes a close look at a particular Scripture and helps the youth understand how to apply biblical principles to the subject of caring for creation.

- **Do Something:** As the name implies, this activity challenges youth to take action, to use what they have learned to make a difference in their congregation, community, and world.

- **Go Forth:** Each session concludes with a prayer and devotion time, during which the youth reflect on what they have learned.

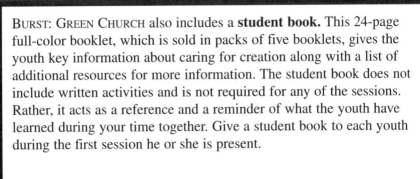

BURST: GREEN CHURCH also includes a **student book.** This 24-page full-color booklet, which is sold in packs of five booklets, gives the youth key information about caring for creation along with a list of additional resources for more information. The student book does not include written activities and is not required for any of the sessions. Rather, it acts as a reference and a reminder of what the youth have learned during your time together. Give a student book to each youth during the first session he or she is present.

How Do I Prepare for Each Session?

Prior to each session, read the introductory article to learn more about each session's topic. Make a note of any questions you have; and do your best to address your questions, either by referring to some of the resources listed at *burst.abingdonyouth.com* or by talking to someone who has expertise in environmental science or in theology.

Review the activity charts provided with each session for notes on the supplies you'll need and what you'll need to do to prepare for specific activities.

If possible, provide for each session environmentally friendly snacks such as fresh, organic, locally grown fruits and vegetables. Consider also serving "shade grown" coffee: coffee that is grown within an ecosystem that doesn't require clearing trees or using chemical pesticides and fertilizers. (Look for one or more of the following certifications on the coffee packaging: "Certified Organic + Certified Shade," "Bird Friendly," or "USDA Organic.")

God saw everything that he had made,
and indeed, it was very good.
—Genesis 1:31a

The LORD *God took the man and put him in the*
garden of Eden to till it and keep it.
—Genesis 2:15

Whose Planet Is This, Anyway?

Each generation gives a gift to the generations that follow: a world that is different from the way it was twenty or thirty years earlier. Sometimes, that gift shows evidence of care. Toxic waste has been cleaned up. Gardens have been planted. Prairies have been set aside and protected. Generations of impoverished, hungry people have been cared for and given a second chance at life.

Other times, that gift shows evidence of last-minute planning, of forgetfulness, of mindlessness. Rivers have been polluted. Farmland has been filled with chemicals, and precious topsoil has blown and washed away. Tribes of people have been virtually wiped out through genocide. Species of birds that once filled the air have disappeared.

All of these environmental crises affect today's teenagers. The job world they will enter will have a greater focus on green technology, on ethical use of resources (including people), on the environmental effects manufactured goods have on people and animals, and on dealing with the effects of rampant consumerism.

Some researchers have predicted that the millennial generation (persons born between 1982 and 1999, give or take a few years) will be the first generation to have a lower standard of living and a shorter life span than the generation before them. In the same way that the millennials are digital natives, completely comfortable with digital technology, many of today's youth will be (or will soon become) the first generation to consistently and daily reflect on and monitor their impact on the environment. They have already grown up with recycle bins in lunchrooms and classrooms and with the subject of greenhouse gases in their science curriculum.

Burst: Green Church

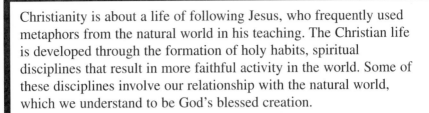

Christianity is about a life of following Jesus, who frequently used metaphors from the natural world in his teaching. The Christian life is developed through the formation of holy habits, spiritual disciplines that result in more faithful activity in the world. Some of these disciplines involve our relationship with the natural world, which we understand to be God's blessed creation.

Our task as leaders and teachers is to help youth to develop holy habits, including those that involve creation care. Many youth already practice earth-friendly disciplines, such as recycling, turning off the water when they brush their teeth, and using green transportation options such as riding a bike or taking the bus. But Christian teens don't always see these habits as practices of faith or expressions of their love of God and neighbor.

An article in *The Journal of Student Ministries* put it this way: "The challenge for those who minister to youth is to help them make connections between earth-friendly habits and discipleship, to help them see going green as an example of Christian holiness. Often the church makes these connections using vague buzz words such as *creation care* and *stewardship*. But what are the biblical and theological underpinnings of these concepts? What other Christian themes are related to our treatment of the environment? And how can we help young people develop green habits that are also holy habits?"

That's what this edition of BURST is all about. In particular, this session challenges youth to not just *claim* the name Christian but to *reclaim* the first role given to humanity: tending and tilling God's garden (**Genesis 1:27-31; 2:8-9, 15**). Reclaiming that role does not deny the importance of other Christian roles and responsibilities; rather, doing so provides a framework for properly seeing the world and our place in it.

This session's title, "Reclaim," has a dual meaning. First, *reclamation* is a term often used for various types of processes that bring an area (land or water) back to a state of usefulness or to its original condition. This is often done to land that has been hurt by strip mining or deforestation or to a river that has been hurt by pollution or erosion. Second, *reclaim* can also mean "to rescue from error and return to a rightful course." Both definitions are important; and both are worthy emphases for youth ministry and for the church, in general. Reclaiming ecosystems so that indigenous species can thrive goes hand in hand with reclaiming our role as stewards of the earth. By reclaiming our environment and our place in it, we honor God, our Creator, Redeemer, and Sustainer.

Some of your youth may live in families that throw away large amounts of trash each week and never think twice about gas mileage; others may come from families that work together to live by the reduce-reuse-recycle mantra. Some may be skeptical of "human-caused global warming." And a few may be leaders of green initiatives at their school.

As you discuss creation care and stewardship, encourage the youth to be honest with one another, to be nonjudgmental in their conversations, and to encourage one another to take steps toward greater awareness of their impact on the environment. If we, as Christians, are going to reclaim our environment, we must first reclaim our commitment to Christian community, cooperation, and love.

In This Session

The youth should come away from this session with an understanding of some basic biblical principles involving care and stewardship of God's creation. In particular, the youth should learn the following key points:

- God created the earth and all that is in it and declared this creation "good."

- God has given humankind the responsibility of tending to creation. Christians today need to reclaim this role.

- Human activity can have very harmful effects on the environment and on the health of humans and other species. As caretakers of creation, we must strive to heal and restore our environment.

- Healing and restoring creation involves changing personal habits; working together as congregations, denominations, or the universal church to make bigger changes; and acting as witnesses for the Creator, who loves the earth and all that is in it.

Getting Ready

As you prepare for this session, read the material on pages 8–11. If you have questions, additional resources are available at *burst.abingdonyouth.com.*

In the days leading up to this session, spend some time reflecting on what it means to be a steward of God's creation. How do you make responsible use of the resources God provides you? Where do you need to improve? How does caring for creation honor the Creator? Identify some ways in which you can lessen your impact on the environment.

Also take some time to review the options under "Do Something: Make [Less of] an Impact" to determine which is most appropriate for your group.

❦ Food Ideas

Provide environmentally friendly snacks such as fresh, organic, locally grown fruits and vegetables. Consider also serving "shade grown" coffee: coffee that is grown within an ecosystem that doesn't require clearing trees or using chemical pesticides and fertilizers. (Look for one or more of the following certifications on the coffee packaging: "Certified Organic + Certified Shade," "Bird Friendly," or "USDA Organic.")

Getting Ready: Read the article on pages 8–10. Also review the following activities and gather or prepare needed supplies.

ACTIVITIES	SUPPLIES
🕊 **Open Your Eyes: A Sense of Place (15–20 minutes)** **Preparation:** Research the history of your church's property	Sticky notes, pens or pencils; a guest expert is optional
🕊 **Think It Through: Around the Campfire (10–15 minutes)** **Preparation:** Create a fake campfire; brush up on your storytelling skills	Copies of the "Creation Campfire Story 1" and "Creation Campfire Story 2" scripts and materials for a fake campfire
🕊 **Tune In: Our Footprint (20–25 minutes)** **Preparation:** Make copies of the "Our Footprint" handout	Copies of the "Our Footprint" handout and answer key, pens or pencils
🕊 **Do Something: Make [Less of] an Impact (15 minutes)**	Supplies depend on the option and project you choose.
🕊 **Go Forth: Live as a Caretaker (10 minutes)**	A ball of string

Open Your Eyes: A Sense of Place

Try to find out as much as you can about what the land your church building sits on was like a century ago. This might be easy if your church is in a rural area; but if it's in a city, you may have to do a bit of research or consult an expert. If your church archives has any pictures that show the groundbreaking ceremony, they may give you some helpful insight.

> **You will need:** sticky notes and pens or pencils. If you have invited a guest expert, ask him or her to help with this activity.

Unless the weather is bad, take the youth outside. Gather in a space that provides the best view of the church property. (If the weather is especially bad, find the best window from which to survey the land.)

Ask the youth to use their imagination and make an educated guess about what the church property might have looked like before it was paved, planted, and built on. Give them a minute to simply observe the topography, the plant life, and any other clues. Then invite the youth to talk about what they think it was like. Once all of the youth have had a chance to describe their visions, tell them the information that you gathered about what the land was like a century ago.

Have the group form a tight circle, facing inward. Then ask the youth to turn 180 degrees so that they are facing outward. As you walk around the circle, say, "I wanted you to think about the space where we meet, because it's a starting point for thinking about how so much of God's creation has changed as a result of human activity. For the next six weeks, we're going to take a hard look at how each of us can better care for God's earth by making small and big changes to the way we live."

To start, ask the youth to name some of the environmental issues that concern them most. Then say each of the following sentences, inviting the youth to complete the sentences, responding as answers come to mind.

• When it comes to our environment, the thing that concerns me most is _____.

• When I hear about major environmental problems in the world, I respond by _____.

14

• In ten years, if humankind continues living as we do now, I think that the world will be _____.

Think It Through: Around the Campfire

If your space does not have shades or curtains, and it will not be dark outside during your meeting time, try to find a way to darken your room. Or find an alternate room that is dark. Create a fake campfire with logs or wood blocks, orange fabric or tissue paper, and flashlights or light a candle. (If you can meet outside, you might be able to use an actual campfire. However, before you do, be sure to check fire regulations in your area.)

Have the youth circle around the "campfire" and darken the room. Tell the youth to imagine that they are ancient Israelites from a small village. Explain that the ancient Israelites would gather together to tell and listen to the stories of their ancestors and their relationship with God.

> **You will need** the "Creation Campfire Story 1" and "Creation Campfire 2" scripts from *burst.abingdon youth.com* and materials to create a fake campfire (wood blocks, orange fabric or tissue paper, and flashlights or a candle).

Read aloud the "Creation Campfire Story 1" script from *burst.abingdonyouth.com,* or read aloud **Genesis 1:1–2:4** from *THE MESSAGE.* Then ask:

• What did you hear in this story that you hadn't expected?

• What, do you think, did this story tell the ancient Israelites about God and God's creation?

• What does this story tell us about humankind's role within creation?

• In what ways have we abused our responsibility to "take charge" over the earth?

• God declared that all of creation is "good." How should this affect our relationship with the world around us?

Reclaim

As time permits, read aloud the "Creation Campfire Story 2" script from *burst.abingdonyouth.com,* or read aloud **Genesis 2:4-15** from the NRSV. Then ask:

- What did you hear in this story that you hadn't expected?

- What, do you think, did this story tell the ancient Israelites about God and God's creation?

- God's creation is described as a beautiful garden, and the first commandment given to humanity is to be gardeners. What does it mean for us today to be gardeners of God's creation?

Note: This discussion of the Bible's creation narratives may raise questions about what science has discovered regarding the origin of our universe and the origin and development of life on earth. These questions often are commonly considered part of a debate between creation and evolution (although creation and evolution need not be mutually exclusive). The website *burst.abingdonyouth.com* offers some resources for addressing these questions, but try not to spend too much time discussing the science of creation. Instead, affirm that, regardless of what mechanisms God uses, God has created our planet and universe and that God loves creation, having declared it "good" (**Genesis 1:31**). For that reason, we all have an obligation to honor God's creation.

Conclude this activity by saying something like: "Well, we can't sit around this campfire forever. We've got work to do as God's gardeners."

Tune In: Our Footprint

In recent years global warming and climate change have become hot topics. Ask the youth what they have heard about these topics. Interject as needed with some of the following information:

> **You will need:** copies of the "Our Footprint" handout and its answer key from *burst.abingdon youth.com,* pens or pencils

- "Global warming" refers to the idea that the planet's overall temperature is rising due to an increase in greenhouse gases. The term "climate change" refers

16

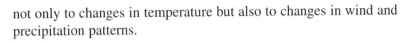

not only to changes in temperature but also to changes in wind and precipitation patterns.

• Greenhouse gases are responsible for trapping radiation from the sun and keeping the planet at a warm temperature. (Without them the earth would be frigid and very uncomfortable.) Significant increases and decreases in the amount of these gases in the atmosphere can have an effect on the planet's climate. Greenhouse gases include water vapor, methane, and carbon dioxide, among others. The amount of carbon dioxide in the atmosphere has increased substantially since the Industrial Revolution.

• The term "carbon footprint" refers to the amount of greenhouse gas, and specifically carbon dioxide, emissions that a person or institution is responsible for. Burning fossil fuels, such as coal and petroleum, is a leading cause of increased carbon dioxide emissions. Ways to shrink one's carbon footprint include using less electricity and gas and switching to more fuel efficient means of transportation.

Say: "Concerns about the amount of greenhouse gases that humans are putting into the atmosphere and the effect of increased greenhouse gas emissions on our climate have caused many people to examine the size of their carbon footprint. But shrinking one's carbon footprint is an act of good stewardship regardless of its effect on the planet's temperatures and weather patterns. By burning fewer fossil fuels, we conserve valuable nonrenewable resources, improve the quality of the air we breathe, and save money that could be put to better use in service of God and others. Our carbon footprint is one (but by no means the only) measure of how faithfully we care for God's creation."

Hand out copies of the "Our Footprint" worksheet from *burst.abingdonyouth.com* and ask the youth to complete this worksheet individually or in small groups. Give them plenty of time to work then go over the answers using the answer key provided (also at *burst.abingdonyouth.com*). Ask the youth to talk about what they learned from this activity about ways in which they can be better stewards of the earth's resources

Do Something: Make [Less of] an Impact

Choose one of the following activities based on your available resources:

Option 1: Have the youth calculate their carbon footprint, using one of the calculators or worksheets available through *burst.abingdonyouth.com*. For some of the items on the calculator or worksheet, such as home electricity and gas usage, youth will

> **You will need** supplies for whatever option and project you choose.

need to make rough estimates or wait to complete their calculations when they get home. Alternatively, work together to calculate the carbon footprint for your church building. If you choose to do this, you should gather information about gas and electricity usage beforehand. (If your church has a van or bus, try to get mileage information as well.)

After the youth have completed their calculations (or have completed as much as possible with the available information), discuss ways that you can reduce your footprint in the coming week and in the coming year.

Option 2: Denominational actions. Do some research to determine what your denomination has to say about environmental issues and what things your denomination—or groups or congregations within your denomination—are doing to protect God's creation. Links to resources for some denominations are available at *burst.abingdonyouth.com*. Discuss ways that the youth can live out the denomination's teachings on the environment or participate in denominational efforts to protect the environment.

Option 3: Church beautification. Improve the ground around our near your church by picking up trash, pulling weeds from flower gardens, raking leaves, or doing another season-appropriate service project. As you work together talk about other ways in which you can tend and till God's great garden.

Option 4: Encourage others in your community to reclaim their role as stewards of God's creation. Help them better understand how their actions have an effect on the environment. Show them how to calculate their carbon footprint (see Option 1) and how to reduce

their carbon footprint. Host an event at your church, rent a booth at a fair or festival, or use the Internet to get your message to a larger audience. Additional resources for this option are available at *burst.abingdonyouth.com.*

Go Forth: Live as a Caretaker

Gather the youth into a circle. (Include yourself in the circle as well.) Hold on to one end of the ball of string and toss the ball to someone across the circle. Ask the person

You will need a ball of string.

who catches the ball to hold on to the string and toss the ball to someone else. Continue this until every person is holding on to the string and a web has been created. Then have the final person to catch the ball toss the ball back to you.

Say: "Sometimes you'll hear people talk about the web of life and how everything and everyone is interconnected. The health and well-being of any one species relies on the health and well-being of several other species and of the planet itself. So it's very important that we faithfully follow God's instructions to care for creation. We're going to unravel this artificial web we've created and depart to go care for the web of life in which we live. When the ball of string comes back to you, say one thing that you intend to do, starting this week, to heal and care for creation then throw the ball back to the person who originally threw it to you."

Throw the ball of string back to the person who threw it to you and have each of the youth do the same. When the web is completely undone, say a prayer thanking God for the gift of creation and asking God for wisdom and guidance as we seek to be faithful stewards of the world in which we live.

*In the seventh year there shall be a sabbath
of complete rest for the land, a sabbath for
the LORD: you shall not sow your field
or prune your vineyard.*
—Leviticus 25:4

Do Less to Do More

Think for a moment about the communication tool or electronic
media you use or prefer most to keep in touch with people and get
information. Now imagine that you were told by your doctor that, in
order to increase the quality of your life, you must refrain from using
that communication tool or technology one day every week. Close
your eyes, and reflect for a while on how you would feel. (Really.
Please do it.)

Did you imagine that you would feel anxious? that if you were to
follow doctor's orders, you would lose touch with people or would
miss something important? Did you feel anger that the doctor had the
gaul to give you such a ridiculous prescription? Or did you imagine
that you would feel relief, because you would enjoy the break and the
excuse to take it?

Any conversation about how we can better be stewards of creation
must start with the Creator. **Genesis 1** tells us that, after six days of
creating the heavens and earth, our Creator set aside the seventh day
as a sabbath and rested.

The word *sabbath* has at its root a word that means "to desist or
stop." But sabbath isn't just about taking a break or resting up after a
long week of work. Rather, sabbath rest refocuses our lives and gives
greater purpose to the work that we do.

In North America today, keeping the sabbath is considered
countercultural. While older adults remember a world where much
commercial activity ceased on Sundays, younger generations have
grown up in a world where malls, stores such as Walmart and Target,
and fast-food restaurants are not only open on Sundays but also do

20

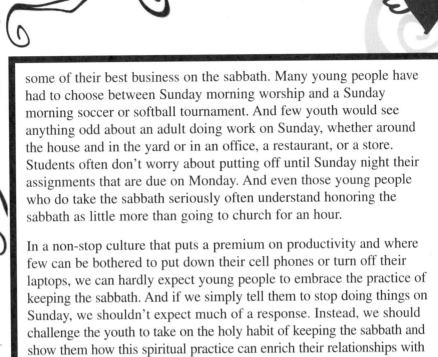

some of their best business on the sabbath. Many young people have had to choose between Sunday morning worship and a Sunday morning soccer or softball tournament. And few youth would see anything odd about an adult doing work on Sunday, whether around the house and in the yard or in an office, a restaurant, or a store. Students often don't worry about putting off until Sunday night their assignments that are due on Monday. And even those young people who do take the sabbath seriously often understand honoring the sabbath as little more than going to church for an hour.

In a non-stop culture that puts a premium on productivity and where few can be bothered to put down their cell phones or turn off their laptops, we can hardly expect young people to embrace the practice of keeping the sabbath. And if we simply tell them to stop doing things on Sunday, we shouldn't expect much of a response. Instead, we should challenge the youth to take on the holy habit of keeping the sabbath and show them how this spiritual practice can enrich their relationships with God and neighbor and can have a positive effect on their health and the health of the world in which they live. Sabbath frees us from the endless cycle or production and consumption and gives us an opportunity to reassert God's centrality in our lives. As Scripture tells us, the sabbath day is a day for renewal and restoration of all of creation.

Scripture has a lot to say about keeping the sabbath. **Genesis 2:3** tells us that the sabbath day is "blessed" (highly favored) and "hallowed" (set apart). In **Exodus 20:8,** God commands everyone in Israel—including residents from other lands, children, and livestock—to "Remember the sabbath, and keep it holy." **Matthew 12:8** teaches us that the "Son of Man is lord of the sabbath," which means that all of the other things that compete for our attention are not. In **Mark 2:27,** Jesus says, "The sabbath was made for humankind, and not humankind for the sabbath." The sabbath is a gift not a burden.

You may be wondering, "Why all this talk about the sabbath in a study about caring for creation?" The connection isn't obvious at first. But as Wayne Muller, founder of the organization Bread for the Journey, writes, "The Sabbath was born with the creation of the earth, so Sabbath time beats in intimate synchronicity with the rhythms of nature" (Wayne Muller, *Sabbath,* page 81). Sabbath-keeping reconnects us with the rest of creation.

In the bustle of everyday life, as we hurry from one obligation to the next, we tend to lose sight of how our lives depend on the world around us. We scarf down fast-food meals on our way from volleyball practice to piano lessons, without giving any thought to who grew, picked, processed, and prepared the food. If we don't finish a sandwich, we throw it out, without giving any thought to the work that went into growing and harvesting the tomatoes, cleaning the lettuce, or baking the bread. We grab large wads of napkins and handfuls of condiment packets, without thinking about what will happen to these things when we throw away the extras. The same can be said for the gasoline we use to get from place to place and for the many disposable products we buy and use for the sake of convenience.

Sabbath gives us an opportunity to stop and remember that we— along with everything we buy, sell, eat drink, touch, or use—are part of God's creation. Sabbath allows us to step away from the cycle of consumption and waste and to think about the things we consume, where they come from, and where they will go. Sabbath is an occasion to simplify and to make do with less.

When we take sabbath rest seriously, we also allow our earth to rest. (**Leviticus 25:3-7** speaks of a sabbath year, in which the land is allowed to rest.) We make more careful use of the earth's resources, we create less trash that will end up in landfills, we better appreciate the beauty of God's creation, and we take on a sane and sustainable way of living that allows all of God's children and creatures to thrive.

In This Session

Youth should come away from this session with an understanding of some basic biblical principles involving care and stewardship of God's creation. In particular, youth should learn the following key points:

- God instructs us to "Remember the sabbath day, and keep it holy" (**Exodus 20:8**). Keeping the sabbath improves our mental, physical, and emotional health; and it can also have a positive impact on the environment.

- Our culture tells us that "more is more," but Scripture illustrates that "less is more." We find abundance not by accumulating material things but by putting our full trust in God.

- While God first gave the laws about the sabbath to the ancient Israelites, the laws extended to foreigners living among the Israelites, the Israelites' servants, livestock, and even the land on which the people lived and worked.

- The sabbath is an excellent opportunity to honor our Creator and creation by refraining from the cycle of consumption and production that leads to unnecessary waste and pollution.

Getting Ready

As you prepare for this session, read the material on pages 20–23. If you have questions, additional resources are available at *burst.abingdonyouth.com*.

In the days leading up to this session, spend some time reflecting on ways that you could reduce (or ways that you have already reduced). These might involve using less water or energy or creating less waste. Think of opportunities you have on a daily or weekly basis to use fewer resources or to use resources more wisely. Think about how putting fewer pollutants into the air can improve people's respiratory health; think about the benefits of conserving an increasingly scarce resource like clean water; and think about how your spiritual health will improve as you let go of material things and put your full trust in God.

Much of this session involves keeping the sabbath. Sabbath-keeping isn't valued much in our culture, which is so focused on productivity. Even many Christians dismiss the fourth commandment in order to have one more day to get things done. Help youth to see keeping the sabbath as a benefit, not a burden. Show them that the sabbath is an opportunity for refreshment and for reorienting oneself toward God. Help them see that honoring the sabbath will have a positive impact on the other six days of the week.

⏱ Food Ideas

Provide environmentally friendly snacks such as fresh, organic, locally grown fruits and vegetables. Consider also serving "shade grown" coffee: coffee that is grown within an ecosystem that doesn't require clearing trees or using chemical pesticides and fertilizers. (Look for one or more of the following certifications on the coffee packaging: "Certified Organic + Certified Shade," "Bird Friendly," or "USDA Organic.")

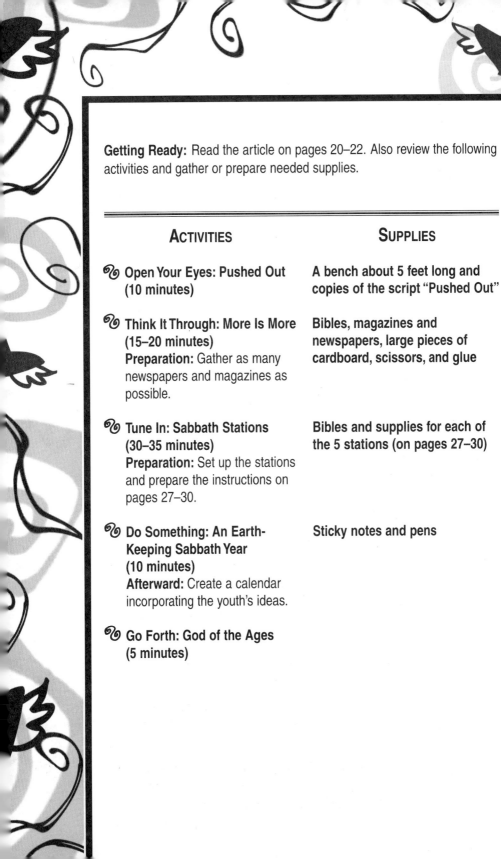

Getting Ready: Read the article on pages 20–22. Also review the following activities and gather or prepare needed supplies.

ACTIVITIES	SUPPLIES
❧ **Open Your Eyes: Pushed Out** (10 minutes)	A bench about 5 feet long and copies of the script "Pushed Out"
❧ **Think It Through: More Is More** (15–20 minutes) **Preparation:** Gather as many newspapers and magazines as possible.	Bibles, magazines and newspapers, large pieces of cardboard, scissors, and glue
❧ **Tune In: Sabbath Stations** (30–35 minutes) **Preparation:** Set up the stations and prepare the instructions on pages 27–30.	Bibles and supplies for each of the 5 stations (on pages 27–30)
❧ **Do Something: An Earth-Keeping Sabbath Year** (10 minutes) **Afterward:** Create a calendar incorporating the youth's ideas.	Sticky notes and pens
❧ **Go Forth: God of the Ages** (5 minutes)	

Open Your Eyes: Pushed Out

Recruit volunteers for an improvisational skit, hand each volunteer a copy of the "Pushed Out" script from *burst.abingdonyouth.com,* and assign parts. (As many as 11 people, or as few as 4, may participate in the skit.)

> **You will need** a bench about 5 feet long and copies of the script "Pushed Out."

Begin the skit with the God character sitting on the bench. Add the other characters one at a time. At some point, God will likely be pushed off the bench and ignored. Following the skit, ask:

• In what ways does this skit illustrate our priorities and the ways that we push God out of our daily lives?

• What other important things tend to get "pushed off the bench"?

Say: "Instead of living a life where several different things compete for space on the bench, we should live a life where God sits on the bench and everyone else gathers around. We should look to God to guide all that we do and all of the decisions we make. In this session we'll look at how putting God at the center of our lives influences our decisions about what we buy and use."

Think It Through: More Is More?

Beforehand, gather as many magazines and newspapers as possible. (Check with libraries that have magazine giveaway bins or with members of the congregation.) This activity is a great way to reuse old periodicals.

> **You will need** Bibles, as many magazines and newspapers as possible, large scissors, pieces of cardboard, and glue.

Divide the group into two teams; and give each team a stack of magazines and newspapers, a large piece of cardboard, scissors, and glue.

Ask: "Have you ever heard people say that 'less is more'? What do people mean by that?" (*This message suggests that we can make do with less.*)

Then say: "We rarely hear the statement 'more is more,' but that is the philosophy behind a lot of the advertising we see and hear. Many ads try to convince us that buying something new will bring fulfillment."

26

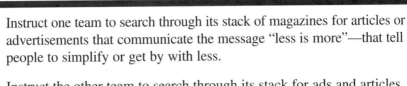

Instruct one team to search through its stack of magazines for articles or advertisements that communicate the message "less is more"—that tell people to simplify or get by with less.

Instruct the other team to search through its stack for ads and articles that communicate the message "more is more"—that tell people that buying something new (and something that they likely don't need) will make them happy. Have the groups cut out and make a stack of the examples that they find.

Give the teams about 5 minutes to work, then ask them to pick out the five best items that they found and to put these on the top of their stacks. Compare the size of the two stacks, then ask each team to present its five best items. Pass around these ten items (five from both groups), and ask the youth to think about which ad or article grabs their attention most.

Then ask volunteers to read aloud the following Scriptures:

- **Exodus 16:9-30**   **Matthew 6:19-21**
- **Matthew 6:25-33**   **Luke 9:1-3**
- **Luke 12:13-21**

Ask:

- What do these Scriptures tell us about getting by with less?

- What are the dangers of accumulating a bunch of stuff that we don't need? (The word *stuff* includes not only material possessions but also media and activities.)

- How easy is it to avoid filling your life with more stuff?

Tune In: Sabbath Stations

Beforehand, set up the five stations described below. If possible, set up these stations in a room other than your normal meeting space. You can print out the station instructions from *burst.abingdonyouth.com* or write the instructions (included below) onto a sheet of paper. If possible, print or write the instructions on the back of a sheet of paper that has already been used.

Say: "Around the room you'll find 5 stations, each of which involves the theme of sabbath rest. Spread out and silently read and follow the instructions for each station. If a station is full, move onto another station and come back to the station you skipped."

Give the youth 25 minutes to visit the stations. Ring a bell (or tap a partially filled glass of water with a spoon) every 5 minutes to give the youth an idea of how much time is left. Since these stations invite personal reflection, encourage the youth to work alone and silently.

Here are the instructions for each of the stations:

Station 1: Exodus 20:8-11

This passage is from the Ten Commandments, which Moses delivered to the Hebrew people in the wilderness. We are to take a day of rest because God did. Resting on the sabbath is such a big deal that it was one of God's first commandments to the Hebrews. Notice how the commandment begins: "Remember." God asks us to remember that God rested and to be aware that we too need rest.

> **For Station 1, you will need** paper, markers, white stickers or labels, jute twine, 7 beads (6 green and 1 red) for each person, and scissors.

Use the supplies provided to create one or more reminders of this commandment. You might make stickers that you could add to a calendar, a sign you could hang in your room, or a bracelet with six green beads and one red bead strung onto jute twine. Take these creations with you when you leave this station.

Station 2: Deuteronomy 5:12-15

This passage is from the version of the Ten Commandments found in Deuteronomy. Why were the Hebrew people supposed to observe the Sabbath by not working for a day? According to Deuteronomy, they were to refrain from working because they had been slaves in Egypt, where Pharaoh had forced them to work long days every day. Now that they were free, God wanted to make sure that

> **For Station 2, you will need** a Bible; paper; pens; if possible, provide a bulletin board, and several push pins.

28

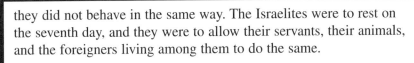

they did not behave in the same way. The Israelites were to rest on the seventh day, and they were to allow their servants, their animals, and the foreigners living among them to do the same.

Using the paper provided, write a letter or short essay, explaining why you think this commandment is still relevant for our culture today. You might write a letter to an elected official or you might write a short essay that you could post on the Internet. Focus on how keeping the sabbath could have a positive effect on God's creation.

Leave your writing at the station, and post it on the bulletin board if one is provided.

Station 3: Leviticus 25:1-7

Sabbath isn't just for people. God instructed the people of Israel to let their fields rest for one year every seven years. Letting the land rest allows the soil to retain its nutrients, because plant matter has time to decompose and enrich the soil.

> **For Station 3, you will need:** a Bible, a piece of fruit for each person that has a rind or peel (such as bananas, oranges, or watermelon slices), a large bowl, and a container labeled "compost."

Take a piece of fruit from the bowl and hold it in your hand. Slowly eat it, savoring its flavor, as you think about the importance of good soil in the world today. When you finish, place the rind or peel in the container labeled "compost." In a compost heap, scraps of food can decay and become organic material that can fertilize future plantings. Compost is an effective way to reuse what God has given us. Say a prayer of thanks for farmers today who grow our food while caring for the land.

Station 4: Leviticus 25:8-17

Leviticus tells us that a special kind of sabbath was to be held in Israel once every 50 years. In that culture, when families became poor, their land was taken by the wealthy and the former owners became slaves. Every 50th year—the Jubilee Year—slaves were released, land was returned to its original owner, and

> **For Station 4, you will need** markers and a large table covered with paper.

Reduce

debts were forgiven. This practice was intended to help restore balance to the economy and to make sure that the people had a just and fair economic system.

Write or draw on the table a representation of what the Jubilee Year might look like in our time. This table is a communal piece of art, so you can build on the contributions of others.

Station 5: Matthew 12:1-14; Mark 2:23-27

In these two Scriptures, Jesus shows how wrong-headed some religious leaders were when it came to the sabbath. They were so strict in their interpretation and application of the sabbath commandment that they had lost sight of its purpose. Jesus said that God created the sabbath for our benefit.

How could the sabbath be a gift to us? How can our keeping the sabbath be a gift to our planet? Write your responses to these questions on the blank side of sheets of gift-wrapping paper then cut them out and tape them to the large gift.

For Station 5, you will need pieces of gift-wrapping paper cut to about 5-by-5 squares, a gift-wrapped box with a bow; transparent tape; and pens.

After 25 minutes at the stations, gather the youth back together. Debrief by asking some of the following questions:

• Prior to this activity, what were your impressions of the sabbath?

• What does your typical Sunday look like?

• What would a person's typical Sunday look like if he or she were to take the sabbath seriously?

• Why is rest so vital to our bodies and to our physical, mental, and emotional health? to creation as a whole?

• Jesus said that we are allowed to heal on the sabbath. How might sabbath be a time for healing the earth?

• What is most challenging about faithfully keeping the sabbath?

Do Something: An Earth-Keeping Sabbath Year

Divide the youth into groups of three or four, and give each group several sticky notes and pens.

> **You will need**
> sticky notes and pens.

Ask the youth to come up with a minimum of four sabbath practices that would help care for or heal God's creation. Examples might be "Go an entire day without turning the lights on in your house" or "Bike to church and back, instead of driving."

Instruct each group to write one such idea on each one of its sticky notes. (You might assign each group a month or season and ask them to come up with ideas that fit the time of year. If you have five or fewer youth, complete this activity as one single group.)

Look through the ideas as a class. Use a calendar and assign each idea to a Sunday during the coming year. Try to fill all of the Sundays. (This may mean repeating some activities or, conversely, assigning more than one activity to a given Sunday.)

Sometime during the following week create, or have a small team of youth volunteers create, a calendar on which of all these ideas are listed on the appropriate Sundays. Distribute the calendar (preferably electronically, to save paper) and challenge the youth to commit to each week's sabbath practice. You might also send out a weekly message reminding the youth of that Sunday's practice.

Go Forth: A Time to Reflect

To close, ask everyone to spend some time in silent prayer, listening to God and reflecting on sabbath rest, on putting God first in their life, and on healing the earth by getting by with less. If possible, spend this time of reflection outdoors.

"Do not store up for yourselves treasures on earth, where moth and rust consume and where thieves break in and steal; but store up for yourselves treasures in heaven. . . . For where your treasure is, there your heart will be also."
—*Matthew 6:19-20a, 21*

Life in a Throwaway World

There may be no segment of the population less prone to reuse resources than teens. Consider for a moment some of the factors that push teens away from reusing resources:

- Their physical development makes continually purchasing clothes a necessity.

- For most teens, the majority of their income is disposable income, money that they may spend in whatever way they choose.

- Teens lead very busy lives, which frequently means that they eat on the run and do not learn to cook from scratch ingredients. Much of the food they eat comes in disposable (and usually non-recyclable) packaging and is eaten with disposable, rather than reusable, napkins and utensils.

- Many of the gadgets that teens enjoy are meant to be replaced when a better model comes along. Properly caring for an MP3 player can be a low priority if a new, better one can be readily purchased.

- Fashion styles change rapidly, and teens are especially sensitive to who is or is not wearing the latest fashions.

- Teens are heavy consumers of ad-supported media, such as television shows, websites, and videogames. The dominant message in advertising is, "Get this now," not "You can get by with what you already have."

- Peer pressure is a greater motivating force for teens than it is for other age groups.

In short, most teens—even those in low-income families—have grown up in a culture where throwing things away and constantly consuming new things is the norm. The average person in the United States generates 4.4 pounds of trash each day. (That's 11,250 pounds of trash generated during the seven teenage years alone.) That trash has enormous consequences for our environment and will continue to have an impact on generations to come.

Over the past several decades, Americans have grown accustomed to throwing things away and buying new things. We've embraced an ethic of wastefulness and are barely conscious of it. This ethic of wastefulness is a spiritual issue. Dependence on God's daily, provisional care for our lives ("Give us this day our daily bread"—**Matthew 6:11**) is easy to reject when one has the financial and technological means to consume more and more.

The natural world is little more than backdrop or scenery for most of us. Because we (like the rich fool of Jesus' parable in **Luke 12**) no longer have to grow our own food or make our own household goods, we are are more likely to understand God's creation as a commodity to be exploited and not as a gift to be tenderly protected. Often we redefine *blessing* to mean *wealth,* rather than *righteousness* and *humility* (**Matthew 5:1-11**). All of this is evidence that we're not in right relationship with God.

But the good news is that is is possible to change our ethic, our way of thinking, and our way of living in the world. First, we must become aware of the depth of the problem and of how the problem relates to our faith. Then we must consciously take responsibility for each choice we make and practice making different choices—guided by the voice of Scripture—until doing so becomes habitual. Finally, we must not be content to make these changes alone; but, instead, we need to develop this ethic in community with those we live, work, and worship with.

Teens are in a stage of moral development in which identity formation is key. Dictionary.com defines *identity* as "the sense of self, providing sameness and continuity in personality over time." This sameness and continuity comes from setting priorities and developing habits. Those of us who minister to youth want these habits and priorities to reflect a life of Christian discipleship. This includes caring for and being good stewards of God's creation. Youth can claim for themselves attitudes and values such as, "I am one who is a wise user of resources," "I am one who considers the way my actions affect others," or "I am a good steward of creation." This session provides an opportunity for youth to "put on" statements like these and to experiment with them in the coming weeks.

In one of the activities for this session, the youth will have the opportunity to reflect on the excuses we make (verbally or implicitly) for our throwaway behavior. They'll contrast these excuses with the good reasons for reusing resources. Most likely, the youth will give reasons that relate to the impact things have on the environment—for example, reusing a water bottle means that less plastic ends up in a landfill. There is nothing wrong with this, but the call for Christians is to make connections to our faith. Help the youth to reflect on the ways that the reuse of finite resources is a wise and faithful habit that demonstrates love for God and neighbor.

In This Session

Youth should come away from this session with an understanding of some basic biblical principles involving being stewards of God's creation by faithfully and responsibly using resources. In particular, youth should learn the following key points:

- We live in a culture that often promotes discarding old things and buying new things. As a result, the average American produces 4.4 pounds of trash each day.

- A lifestyle in which we constantly consume and throw away is not sustainable.

- Scripture tells us that abundance is not about accumulating possessions but about fully giving ourselves to God and living a life of service to God and others. As Christians, we need to remember what it means to be blessed (**Matthew 5:1-11**) and to trust God to provide.

- Reusing is a very effective way to reduce waste. We—as individuals, families, and congregations—need to be mindful of ways that we can reuse items that we would otherwise throw away.

Getting Ready

As you prepare for this session, read the material on pages 32–35. If you have questions, additional resources are available at *burst.abingdonyouth.com.*

In the days leading up to this session spend some time reflecting on ways that you reuse items that you would otherwise throw away. Think and pray also about ways that you could reuse some of the things that end up in your trash can or recycling bin. How might you make use of that empty sour cream tub or that one-side-used handout from last week's Bible study? Reflect on the benefits of reusing things instead of throwing them away and buying new things (less trash in landfills, fewer resources being used to produce new products, and so forth). Also take time to read and reflect on passages such as **Matthew 6:19-21** (treasures in heaven) and **Luke 12:13-21** (the parable of the rich fool) that warn about the dangers of constant consumption.

Food Ideas

Provide environmentally friendly snacks such as fresh, organic, locally grown fruits and vegetables. Consider also serving "shade grown" coffee: coffee that is grown within an ecosystem that doesn't require clearing trees or using chemical pesticides and fertilizers. (Look for one or more of the following certifications on the coffee packaging: "Certified Organic + Certified Shade," "Bird Friendly," or "USDA Organic.")

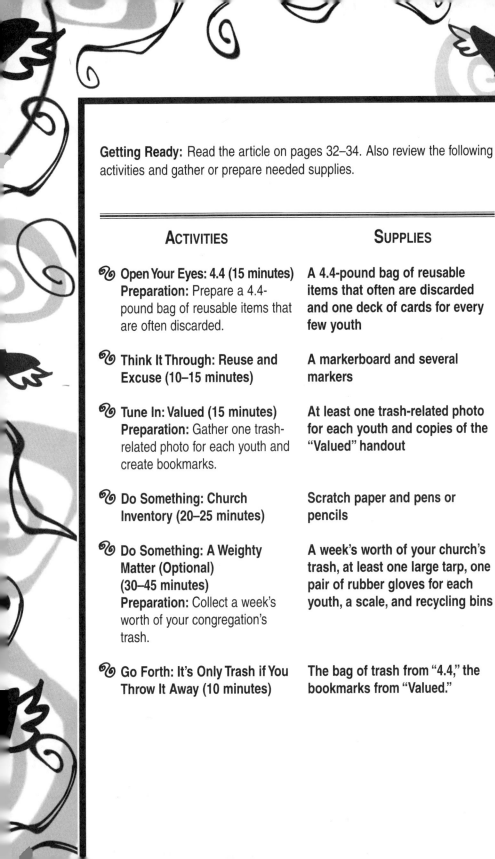

Getting Ready: Read the article on pages 32–34. Also review the following activities and gather or prepare needed supplies.

ACTIVITIES	SUPPLIES
✆ **Open Your Eyes: 4.4 (15 minutes)** **Preparation:** Prepare a 4.4-pound bag of reusable items that are often discarded.	**A 4.4-pound bag of reusable items that often are discarded and one deck of cards for every few youth**
✆ **Think It Through: Reuse and Excuse (10–15 minutes)**	**A markerboard and several markers**
✆ **Tune In: Valued (15 minutes)** **Preparation:** Gather one trash-related photo for each youth and create bookmarks.	**At least one trash-related photo for each youth and copies of the "Valued" handout**
✆ **Do Something: Church Inventory (20–25 minutes)**	**Scratch paper and pens or pencils**
✆ **Do Something: A Weighty Matter (Optional) (30–45 minutes)** **Preparation:** Collect a week's worth of your congregation's trash.	**A week's worth of your church's trash, at least one large tarp, one pair of rubber gloves for each youth, a scale, and recycling bins**
✆ **Go Forth: It's Only Trash if You Throw It Away (10 minutes)**	**The bag of trash from "4.4," the bookmarks from "Valued."**

Open Your Eyes: 4.4

Beforehand, gather a variety of small reusable items from your house or church that add up to a total of 4.4 pounds. Examples might include rags, refillable bottles, old socks, rechargeable batteries, paper used on only one side, old magazines, and (clean) sour cream or margarine tubs. Put everything in a bag so that the items are not visible.

> **You will need** a deck of cards for every few youth and a bag of reusable items that are often discarded and that have a combined weight of 4.4 pounds.

Hand out one deck of cards for every few youth. (Sets of cards from board games will also work. Use cards that you already have access to rather than buying new ones.)

As the youth arrive, divide them into groups of three or four. Ask the groups to spread out. Challenge the groups to build a durable house of cards, one that could survive a light wind. No other supplies may be used (just the cards), and you should not give the groups any additional instructions.

Give the youth about 5 minutes to create their houses of cards. Then allow the groups to (carefully) look at the others groups' creations. Give each house the "breath test" by blowing lightly on it for a few seconds and seeing whether it can withstand the breeze.

Then pass around the bag of reusable items, but instruct the youth not to open it or look inside. Instead, they are to just think about its weight.

Say: "The contents of this bag represent the amount of trash that the average American throws out every single day. Feel it and try to guess the weight of the bag."

After everyone has had a chance to guess the weight, say: "The actual weight is 4.4 pounds. The average person in the United States produces 4.4 pounds of trash per day. That means that, during the average teen's teenage years, he or she produces a total of 11,250 pounds of trash."

Ask:

• What are some of the things that you often contribute to that 4.4-pound average?

38

- Your instruction for this activity was to construct a durable, sustainable house of cards. How durable and sustainable was the house you built? What sorts of things could have destroyed your house?

- How sustainable is a lifestyle in which we throw away 4.4 pounds of trash per day? What sorts of things could destroy this way of life? (*scarcity of important resources, pollution from waste disposal, and so on*)

Think It Through: Reuse and Excuse

Divide a markerboard in half. Label one half "Reuse" and the other "Excuse." Set out several markers.

Instruct the youth to write on the "Reuse" side of the board some reasons to reuse items, benefits of reusing, and common items that can be reused. Instruct them to write on the "Excuse" side some common excuses for not reusing things. Once the youth have written several things on the board, ask the youth to draw lines connecting related ideas. (For example "refillable bottles" might be listed as an item that can be reused; youth may draw lines from "refillable bottles" to any excuse that someone might use for throwing these bottles away.)

> **You will need a** markerboard and several markers.

Give the youth several minutes to work. Then have everyone step back and take a moment to reflect on what they have written and the connections they have made.

Read through some of the reasons for and benefits of reusing. Then read through some of the excuses listed.

Ask:

- What, do you think, is the best reason to reuse things instead of throwing them away?

- Excuses are like little arguments in which we try to convince ourselves or others to do something that we know we shouldn't do (or not to do something that we know we should do). As arguments, which of these excuses are the most persuasive?

- What are some of the holes in these arguments?

- What are some ways that you—along with your friends and peers—could reuse more of the things that you might otherwise throw away and could make fewer excuses for not reusing things?

Tune In: Valued

Beforehand, print or collect several photos related to waste—trash cans, landfills, impoverished children sorting through trash, garbage trucks, and so forth. Fold these photos in half and use them as bookmarks to mark the Scripture passages that the youth will be reading as a part of this activity. Be sure to have at least one bookmark for each youth.

> **You will need**
> photos related to waste (at least one for each youth), Bibles, and copies of the "Valued" handout from *burst.abingdon youth.com*

Distribute Bibles and the "Valued" handout from *burst.abingdonyouth.com* and divide the youth into three groups. Assign each group one of the three Scriptures on the handout (**Matthew 5:1-11; Luke 11:1-4;** and **Luke 12:13-31**). As much as possible, place middle school youth in the **Luke 11:1-4** and **Luke 12:13-31** groups. These Scriptures and their accompanying questions will appeal more to concrete thinkers than the Beatitudes Scripture from Matthew.

Option: Ask a group of older youth to read **Matthew 5:1-11** and **Luke 12:13-31** and to work together to create a current-day parable about faithfully using resources and what it truly means to be blessed.

Do Something: Church Inventory

Hand out scratch paper (that is, paper that is already used on one side) and pens or pencils. Divide the youth into groups of three or four, and instruct each group to tour the church building and to evaluate how well your

> **You will need**
> scratch paper and pens or pencils.

congregation is using and reusing resources. They could look to see whether disposable or reusable cups, dishes, and utensils are used for church meals; whether church bulletins and newsletters are reused or recycled; whether the church is wasting electricity or water; and whether the church has found creative ways to reuse things such as

40

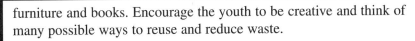

furniture and books. Encourage the youth to be creative and think of many possible ways to reuse and reduce waste.

Give the teams several minutes to do their investigations. Make sure that they do not disrupt other groups that are meeting in the church at the same time. (You might also need to restrict the youth from certain areas, such as offices. However, these may be the rooms that produce the most trash; so let the youth investigate them if it is possible.)

When the youth return, have each team talk about its findings. Keep a list of their observations on a markerboard. (You might list these observations in two columns: "Things We Do Well" and "Things That Need Improvement.")

Focus the youth's attention on the areas that need improvement. Have them identify improvements that could be made immediately and those that might take more time. Ask for volunteers who would be willing to make a presentation to your church's leadership council and/or staff about short-term and long-term changes that might be made. Make arrangements to meet with this group to help them prepare their presentation, and help the group get an audience with your congregation's leadership.

Do Something: A Weighty Matter (Optional)

Beforehand, make arrangements to collect several bags of your church's trash. As much as possible, take the bags out of the trash cans shortly before your meeting time so that you won't have to store the trash. If yours is a small congregation, if the church has a place to store bags of trash, and if you have the blessing of the church staff, consider gathering an entire week's worth of garbage.

> **You will need**
> several bags of your church's trash, at least one large tarp, one pair of rubber gloves for each youth, a scale, and recycling bins.

Ask the youth to come dressed in old clothes and (if possible) to bring a pair of rubber gloves. (Provide extras for those who don't have any.)

Spread out a tarp (outdoors if possible) and dump all of the trash onto the tarp. Have the youth work together to separate the types of trash

into categories such as recyclable plastic, food waste, paper towels, cardboard, and so on. Have the youth make note of anything that could be recycled (and provide containers to collect these materials) or reused (such as for Sunday school crafts, as scrap paper, or for compost.) Provide guidelines for the youth, explaining exactly what materials can be recycled or used as compost. (Local recycling programs vary in terms of what materials they will accept; check with the program in your area. Organic materials such as fruits, vegetables, and egg shells can be composted; some other food waste—such as bread, cooked food, meat, and nuts—cannot. See *burst.abingdonyouth.com* for additional resources on composting.) Use a scale to weigh each category of trash. Then use a calculator to determine what percent (in terms of weight) of the trash is reusable and/or recyclable. Ask for youth volunteers to work together to prepare a brief report for the congregation and to recommend ways to reuse materials that might otherwise be thrown away.

Go Forth: It's Only Trash if You Throw It Away

Open the bag of "trash" that you prepared for the "4.4" activity above. Point out that the items in the bag are not actually trash but are reusable items.

> **You will need**
> the bag of trash from "4.4," the bookmarks from "Valued."

Then distribute the bookmarks you created for "Valued" (above) so that each youth gets one. Have the youth spend a minute in silence, reflecting on the image on their bookmark. Ask the youth to take home their bookmarks as a reminder of God's call to care for creation in the way they use and reuse resources.

Gather everyone into a circle, take one of the items from the bag, and pass it around the circle. As it comes to each person, have that person make a statement of commitment about what he or she will do in the next week to reuse resources and to waste less.

Close with the prayer on page 43.

Creator God, who makes all things new,

Your world is awesome in its diversity, astounding in its complexity, and abundant in its production.

Forgive us for our actions that have led to a reduction in that diversity, though the extinction of species you loved.

Forgive us for our actions that have shown that we have forgotten how complex the environment is and how our actions have far-reaching consequences.

Forgive us for our actions that have taken lightly earth's abundance, for wastefulness and overuse of earth's resources.

We ask you, God, to reuse our lives for the good of others. Make of us a people who are unafraid to live wisely and gently on this planet so that we can hand it on to generations yet to come with the promise that we have cared for your creation. Amen.

Reuse

RECYCLE

All are from the dust, and all turn to dust again.
—Ecclesiastes 3:20b

Before You Throw That Away . . .

Trash is strewn along the path to the summit of Mt. Everest. Thousands of pieces of space debris float in the upper stratosphere. Modern graffiti is scratched into historic natural landmarks. Hypodermic needles and plastic 6-pack rings wash up on ocean shores each morning. These are just a few of the reminders that one of the things humans do well is leave behind a mess wherever they go. Each instance is an indicator that someone did not think through the larger consequences of his or her actions, cared little for generations to come, or felt that he or she had the right to make his or her mark on the world.

In his 2009 book *Ecological Intelligence: How Knowing the Hidden Impacts of What We Buy Can Change Everything,* Daniel Goleman argues that we need to develop human awareness of how things, people, and the earth are linked by learning more about how items are made. Things are not so simple as they may appear; "green" products, such as cotton canvas reusable bags, sometimes require far more resources for their production than their petroleum-based counterparts. Even recycling is not benign; when we recycle we are sometimes reusing toxins and generating new ones. Most of us, though, tell ourselves what playwright Henrik Ibsen called a "vital lie," a story we believe and tell ourselves that covers up a more painful truth. Goleman writes, "When it comes to the full costs of ecological ignorance in the marketplace, we endorse the vital lie that what we don't know or can't see does not matter. In fact, our indifference to the consequences of the sum total of what we buy and do and our unexamined habits as consumers drive a vast number of threats to the environment and to health."

Awareness of this vital lie is one necessary step in making better choices, and books such as Goleman's help individuals become better informed. Ultimately, though, what is essential is the spiritual truths that material things do not provide a meaningful sense of self-worth, that making life worse for others does not make our lives better, and that our time on this planet is tiny when compared with the scope of creation. Although it's a

44

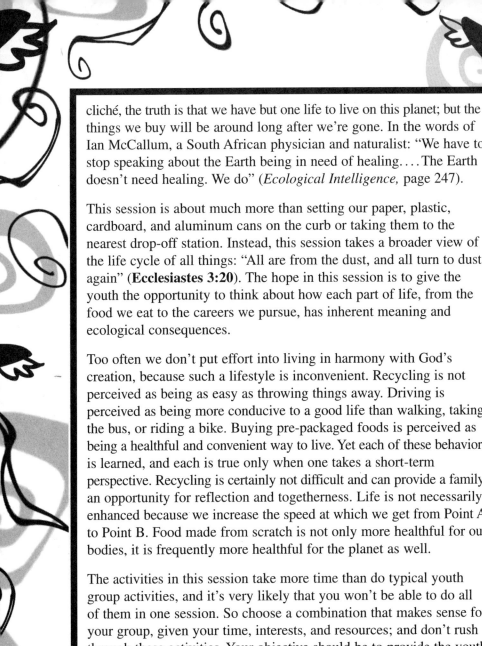

cliché, the truth is that we have but one life to live on this planet; but the things we buy will be around long after we're gone. In the words of Ian McCallum, a South African physician and naturalist: "We have to stop speaking about the Earth being in need of healing.... The Earth doesn't need healing. We do" (*Ecological Intelligence,* page 247).

This session is about much more than setting our paper, plastic, cardboard, and aluminum cans on the curb or taking them to the nearest drop-off station. Instead, this session takes a broader view of the life cycle of all things: "All are from the dust, and all turn to dust again" (**Ecclesiastes 3:20**). The hope in this session is to give the youth the opportunity to think about how each part of life, from the food we eat to the careers we pursue, has inherent meaning and ecological consequences.

Too often we don't put effort into living in harmony with God's creation, because such a lifestyle is inconvenient. Recycling is not perceived as being as easy as throwing things away. Driving is perceived as being more conducive to a good life than walking, taking the bus, or riding a bike. Buying pre-packaged foods is perceived as being a healthful and convenient way to live. Yet each of these behaviors is learned, and each is true only when one takes a short-term perspective. Recycling is certainly not difficult and can provide a family an opportunity for reflection and togetherness. Life is not necessarily enhanced because we increase the speed at which we get from Point A to Point B. Food made from scratch is not only more healthful for our bodies, it is frequently more healthful for the planet as well.

The activities in this session take more time than do typical youth group activities, and it's very likely that you won't be able to do all of them in one session. So choose a combination that makes sense for your group, given your time, interests, and resources; and don't rush through these activities. Your objective should be to provide the youth an opportunity to carefully think about what they value, discern how their actions match their values, and hear the voice of God calling them to serve God's creation in unique ways. The teenage years are an ideal time to choose a life path in which people and the planet are more valued than possessions are.

Recycling itself can be a spiritual practice for youth. Each piece of paper or plastic encountered is a chance for gratitude for the people

Recycle

and resources needed to produce it. Recycling those items is a way to say thanks and to ensure that the work of others has even greater and more long-lasting value. Recycling forces us to be conscious of how much we consume, and it forces us to act intentionally to clean up our own mess. In addition, recycling is a metaphor for our lives. Out of the wasted days of our past, and from the unused potential within each of us, God fashions a new life.

In This Session

Youth should come away from this session with an understanding of some basic biblical principles faithfully and responsibly using the resources God has given us. In particular, youth should learn the following key points:

- While recycling packaging and containers is better than throwing them away, it is best to find ways to avoid buying things with disposable packaging. One way to do this is to prepare more meals from scratch.

- Garbage—particularly plastic—not only accumulates in landfills but also pollutes our oceans. As stewards of God's creation, we must care for the waters and the creatures that inhabit them by reducing the amount of waste that ends up in our oceans.

- Scripture reminds us that our lives on this earth are fleeting. We come from dust, and we will return to dust. Thus we must seize every opportunity to love and serve God and neighbor during our earthly lives. One way to do this is by conserving valuable resources that God created and that future generations will need to survive.

- We must commit to producing less waste by reducing, reusing, and recycling.

Getting Ready

As you prepare for this session, read the material on pages 44–47. If you have questions, additional resources are available at *burst.abingdonyouth.com.*

In the days leading up to this session, think about recycling. What opportunities for recycling are available in your community? Can you leave recyclable materials on your curb to be picked up, or must you take them to a drop-off station? Are there ways that you could reduce or reuse some of the containers and other materials that you often recycle? Think about the benefits of recycling and the consequences of simply throwing things away.

This session isn't strictly about recycling but about being mindful of the things we use and throw away. Conservationists long have touted the "Three *Rs*"—reduce, reuse, and recycle. While each "*R*" is the subject of a separate session in this study, all three have a common objective: producing less waste. It is best if we can reduce by consuming less. But we can't entirely avoid buying new things. So whenever possible, we should find ways to reuse the things we buy after we've used them for their original purpose. And once something such as an article of clothing, a food container, or a rechargeable battery is no longer usable, we should recycle it instead of simply throwing it away.

℁ Food Ideas

Provide environmentally friendly snacks such as fresh, organic, locally grown fruits and vegetables. Consider also serving "shade grown" coffee: coffee that is grown within an ecosystem that doesn't require clearing trees or using chemical pesticides and fertilizers. (Look for one or more of the following certifications on the coffee packaging: "Certified Organic + Certified Shade," "Bird Friendly," or "USDA Organic.")

Getting Ready: Read the article on pages 44–46. Also review the following activities and gather or prepare needed supplies.

ACTIVITIES	SUPPLIES
❧ **Open Your Eyes: Made From Scratch (15 minutes)** **Preparation:** Select a recipe that your youth can make from scratch and gather ingredients for this recipe (preferably ingredients that don't come in disposable packaging).	**Copies of a recipe (see the activity), ingredients for that recipe, and a place to prepare and cook food**
❧ **Think It Through: Great Pacific Garbage Patch (10–20 minutes)** **Preparation:** Look at articles and videos about the Great Pacific Garbage Patch	**Videos and articles about the Great Pacific Garbage Patch, a DVD player or computer with projector, a copy of Disney's** *Wall-E** **on DVD (optional) (See licensing info on page 54.)**
❧ **Tune In: Dust—Life—Dust (15 minutes)**	**Bibles, dust (see the activity), a markerboard and marker, and a CD with the song "Dust in the Wind" (optional) and a CD player**
❧ **Do Something: An Action Plan (15–20 minutes)**	**Markers, paper, pens or pencils, the list from "Great Pacific Garbage Patch" activity**
❧ **Go Forth: The Three** *Rs* **(10 minutes)**	**One-side-used slips of paper, pens or pencils**

Open Your Eyes: Made From Scratch

Beforehand, select a recipe that your youth can make completely from scratch; and buy the ingredients necessary for this recipe. You might choose to have the youth make a coffee cake, a batch of cookies, a loaf of quick bread (not yeast), a pot of soup (a potato soup that isn't made with prepared broth will work), or a pizza. Ideally choose a recipe that can be prepared in 10 minutes or less and that will finish cooking

> **You will need** copies of a recipe, ingredients for that recipe, and a place and cookware to prepare and cook food.

during the time you will be gathered together. Resist the temptation to buy prepared ingredients. (For example, buy a block of cheese at the deli section of a grocery store—not a pre-packaged block of cheese—and use a cheese-grater, instead of buying a package of shredded cheese.) If you have several youth, select a food that could be prepared by a number of small groups (such as quick breads and other baked goods).

Note: Try to get ingredients that are not packaged in plastic. Some may be difficult to find packaged in other ways, but they are often available in bulk at health food stores that allow you to use your own containers. Also, make the recipe so that you can know how to help if needed and how it will taste.

Have all of the ingredients and materials ready and organized when the youth arrive; but leave all of the food preparation for the youth.

As the youth arrive, chat informally with them about the food and food-related habits in their house. What do their meals typically consist of? How well do they know how to cook? Do any of their family members cook entirely from scratch on a regular basis?

Tell the youth that they are going to make some food from scratch. Divide the youth into groups if necessary, then give each group the recipe and allow the group members to work together. Provide assistance only when absolutely necessary. As the youth finish preparing the food, put it on the stove or in the (preheated) oven and have an adult volunteer keep an eye on the food and the baking or cooking time.

Meanwhile, continue the conversation you started earlier. Ask:

• How easy or difficult was it to follow the recipe? How well did everything come together?

- What sorts of things does your family cook from scratch? What sorts of things do you never make from scratch? Why?

- What, do you think, does cooking from scratch have to do with caring for creation?

Think It Through: Great Pacific Garbage Patch

Ask the youth whether they are familiar with the Great Pacific Garbage Patch. If they are familiar, ask them to tell what they know about it. Otherwise, explain that the Great Pacific Garbage Patch is a massive patch of garbage that has accumulated in the Pacific Ocean. Videos and articles related to the Great Pacific Garbage Patch are available at *burst.abingdonyouth.com.* If possible show one of these videos and allow the youth to react.

You will need a markerboard and markers, videos and articles about the Great Pacific Garbage Patch, and a DVD player or a computer with projector. A DVD of *Wall-E* is optional. If you choose this option, be sure to have a license (see page 54) to show the video to your group.

Then ask:

- Were you surprised to learn that so much garbage is floating in the ocean? Were you surprised by the types of trash in the Garbage Patch?

- How might you be contributing to the Great Pacific Garbage Patch and other ocean pollution?

- Think about the food you eat each day. How much of this food is packaged in disposable plastic?

Then ask the youth to brainstorm some ways to reduce the amount of plastic that we, as a congregation and community, use and throw away. This could involve learning where and how to buy items that aren't packaged in plastic; educating your congregation and community about where and how to recycle plastic containers; or finding alternatives to disposable plastics. Contribute some ideas of your own and record all the ideas on a markerboard.

Option: Show some of the opening scenes from the popular 2008 movie *Wall-E.* Start at around 1:20 (shot of the entire earth) and go

Recycle

51

until either 8:10 (Wall-E exits his home) or 11:10 (Wall-E puts the plant in the shoe). Then ask:

• What, do you think, were the creators of *Wall-E* trying to say about what humans have done and are doing to the planet?

• What items did you notice in this scene that you hadn't thought of as trash before?

Tune In: Dust—Life—Dust

Ask the youth to use an index finger to swipe a dusty shelf, window sill, TV, or other surface in your room. (If your room is mostly dust-free, you may need to bring in a dusty item.)

Option: Play the classic rock song "Dust in the Wind," which was written and originally recorded by Kansas and more recently recorded by other bands, as the youth look at the dust they have collected on their finger.

> **You will need**
> Bibles, dust (see the activity), a markerboard, a marker, and a CD with the song "Dust in the Wind" (optional) and a CD player.

Ask:

• What is dust, anyway?

Explain that the dust in our homes, schools, and workplaces consists largely of dead skin particles, as well as human and animal hair, fibers from carpets and furniture, and assorted minerals.

Ask volunteers to read aloud the following Scriptures:

   • **Genesis 2:7**   • **Genesis 3:19**

   • **Psalm 90:2-6**   • **Ecclesiastes 3:20**

Say: "As Christians, we know that we have eternal life through Christ. But these Scriptures remind us that our earthly lives are fleeting. When we consider the age of the universe, our life spans are tiny by comparison. We have to make the most of the time we have."

Read aloud **Mark 12:28-31.** Then say: "Jesus tells us that the two greatest commandments are to love God and to love our neighbor. In

52   Burst: Green Church

the short time that we have on earth, we must seize every opportunity to serve God and neighbor. One of the ways we do this is by being good stewards of God's creation. Caring for the earth honors God and shows love for all those who will rely on our planet and its natural resources after we have returned to dust. As Christians, we believe that God, through the death and resurrection of Christ and the ongoing work of the Holy Spirit, is working to redeem creation and bring it to fulfillment. By caring for the earth and making responsible use of its resources, we participate in this work of redemption."

Ask the students to spread out. Write the sentence starters (below) on a markerboard where everyone can see them. Ask the youth to spend a few minutes in silence reflecting on these statements:

• Caring for creation involves . . .

• At the end of my life, I would like to say that my relationship with God's creation has been . . .

• It is difficult for me to be mindful of God's creation when . . .

• I am in a position to heal and protect the earth by . . .

• I can develop daily creation-care habits such as . . .

Do Something: An Action Plan

Direct the youths' attention back to the list of ways to reduce the amount of plastic we use and throw away (from "Great Pacific Garbage Patch," above). Distribute markers and ask each person to put his or her initials next to one idea that he or she would like to follow through with.

> **You will need**
> markers, paper, pens or pencils, and the list from "Great Pacific Garbage Patch" activity.

Have the youth form groups based on their choices. Youth who are alone may work alone, pair with another individual, or switch groups.

Set out paper and pens or pencils. Encourage the youth to come up with a specific plan to follow through with the idea they've chosen. Tell them to create timelines, set additional times to meet, and determine whom else they need to involve. Some groups will likely finish quickly. Others

will need more time to plan their projects. Encourage groups that finish quickly to think of ways to expand on their plans or to help other groups.

Give the groups about 10 minutes to plan, then have a representative from each group briefly describe what his or her group plans to do.

In the coming weeks, hold the groups accountable to these projects by reminding them of their commitments and checking up on their progress.

Option: If you would prefer to do a project as a full group, selling reusable bags is a great fundraiser. Information on this and other fundraisers is available at *burst.abingdonyouth.com.*

Go Forth: The Three *Rs*

Say: "This study on greening the church is based on 6 *Rs: reclaim, reduce, reuse, recycle, repent,* and *rejoice.* But three of these *Rs—reduce, reuse,* and *recycle*—have been used in conservation campaigns for years. Now that we've learned about reducing, reusing, and recycling, let's close by setting some personal goals related to these three *Rs.*"

> **You will need**
> one-side-used slips of paper and pens or pencils.

Hand out slips of paper that are obviously being reused (such as backs of old worship bulletins or Sunday school handouts). Instruct each person to write on the slip of paper three practices that they can take on in the coming week: one involving reducing the amount of things they buy and use, one involving finding creative ways to reuse what they have instead of buying new things, and one involving recycling. Check on these commitments in the coming weeks.

> **Note:** *When you show home videocassettes or DVDs to a group of learners, you need to obtain a license. You can get a public performance license from Christian Video Licensing International (1-888-771-2854 or cvli.com). The license can cost over $100. Check with your church to see whether an umbrella license has already been obtained. Through conferences, jurisdictions, dioceses, and other structures, many denominations secure licenses for their churches to show films.*

Give the youth several minutes to think of practices they will take on. Then close with the prayer below (responses in boldface). Write the student responses on a markerboard.

We confess that we have misused God's creation.

God our Creator, we are sorry
for the times when we have used your gifts carelessly,
and acted ungratefully.

We enjoy the fruits of the harvest
but sometimes forget that you have given them to us.

We often ignore the cry of the needy and hungry
and do not care enough for the world you have made.

We store up goods for ourselves alone
as if there were no God and no heaven.

Hear this good news: In the name of Christ,
you are forgiven.
In the name of Christ, you are forgiven.

Give us a reverence for the earth as your own creation
that we may use its resources rightly
in the service of others
and to your honor and glory.
Glory to God! Amen.

Recycle

REPENT

"Repent, and believe in the good news."
—Mark 1:15

Turn and Walk Down Earth's Way

Author's reflection:

> During the week that I wrote this lesson, I dug out and planted two new perennial gardens; and I took in the recyclables that had accumulated on my front porch for the past several months. I have often joked that I could kill a plastic plant, so putting in two new gardens may turn out to be a futile endeavor. But for me, these gardening efforts are one way to repent for living in a way that is too often disconnected from the natural world. With each shovel of dirt I moved, I offered a simple prayer: "Forgive me, Creator God, for not tending and tilling your garden."
>
> I am fortunate to live in a community with a recycling center that accepts nearly everything, and my wife and I dispose of as little trash as possible as a result. The tubs of glass, plastic, paper, newspaper, paperboard, magazines, and other items must have collectively weighed between 200 and 250 pounds. As I loaded the empty bins and boxes back into my car, I found myself amazed—and ashamed—by the volume of material I had caused to be produced.

The trash produced by the convenience-oriented lifestyle many of us enjoy has several unseen consequences. Glass—a fully reusable and recyclable product—requires harmful chemicals and a great deal of energy for its manufacture. Plastic, as we saw in our last session, too

56

often ends up in our oceans or local bodies of water; and biochemists say that we all carry plastic-related chemicals in our bodies. The waste that is produced when products are made in other countries is not shipped overseas along with the gadgets and trinkets and clothing but, instead, stays in countries that are often ill-equipped to deal with it.

And sometimes, when we think that we are helping the environment by using fuel made from renewable food crops, such as corn, we end up inflating food prices, making some foods unaffordable for impoverished populations.

We need to take into consideration how our actions and habits have global consequences, with the poor and the natural world usually paying the highest price. We have lived lives out of balance and need to individually and collectively repent and turn in a new direction.

Repentance is one of those "religious" words that many Christians detest. Attendance at Ash Wednesday services is certainly not equal to attendance on Christmas Eve. Often we associate repentance with people wearing sandwich boards that read, "Repent! The end is near." Or we may associate it with street preachers, tent revivals, and traditions that over-emphasize guilt and sin at the expense of grace and mercy.

Yet many Jewish rituals were connected with repentance, such as the purification baths, which are commonly found at ancient archeological sites. Repentance was the core message of John the Baptist; and Jesus' first public message was, "Repent, and believe in the good news" (**Mark 1:15**). The Greek word that we translate as *repent* literally means "turn around, to stop going in the direction one is traveling and go another way." In the Old Testament, the concept of repentance is typically indicated with the words *turn* or *return.* (See **Ezekiel 18:32** and **Isaiah 55:6-7.**)

According to theologian Walter Brueggemann, repentance is the act of turning away from sin and resuming one's walk on the path of obedience to God. He explains that repentance isn't just a one-time act. Rather, it is a long-term commitment to act differently—a resolution to live according to God's will. Repentance is a restoration of our covenantal relationship with God and neighbor. It is the spark that causes one to burn with new passion for the way of shalom, the path of Christ.

Repent

The story the youth will explore this week is the story of Jonah. It's a story that many young people are familiar with, but teens should know that Jonah is about much more than a big fish. (If it has been a while since you have read the whole story, do so before your session. It's quite short.) God tells Jonah to go to Nineveh—that is, to the capital of the wicked and powerful Assyrian Empire. Jonah tries to run away. Eventually (in that well-known part of the story), he gets back on track and tells the Ninevites to repent. Amazingly, they do so. Jonah is really upset with God for not destroying those evil Ninevites; and an object lesson ensues that involves a shady bush that is destroyed by a worm, leaving Jonah angry and sunburned. In the end, God's words (which end the story) are remarkable: "And should I not be concerned about Nineveh, that great city, in which there are more than a hundred and twenty thousand persons who do not know their right hand from their left, and also many animals?" (**Jonah 4:11**).

The story of Jonah expanded the ancient Jewish theology of God. God not only loved the people of Israel, but God deeply loved all people—including non-Jews—and all other creatures. This was a huge leap of understanding for the people of Jonah's time. In our own time, we may find it much easier to believe that God loves all people and that God loves creation. What is far more difficult for youth (and adults) is responding to God's love by demonstrating our love for our neighbors and for all creatures. We express this love, in part, by caring for the environment: making responsible use of the resources that all people and animals need to live and protecting fragile ecosystems that other creatures call home. Like the Ninevites, we do need to hear God's call to repentance of our ways; like Jonah, we need to repent of our assumption that we hold God's special favor.

Now, a reality check: Repentance of our harmful environmental actions is really, really hard; and we cannot change overnight or alone. (Remember that repenting is more than merely confessing. It also requires us to turn away from our sins and head in a different direction.) Instead, your session is a call to youth to begin that walk together in a new direction. Small changes can be made immediately; habits can be formed over time; career choices can be altered; pressure can be exerted on governments and corporations (and families and congregations) to change. It is crucial for us as individuals to repent, but it is also time for us all to go forth like Jonah and call others to repentance.

In This Session

Youth should come away from this session with an understanding of repentance and with ideas for how they—and the entire congregation—can repent of ways in which they have not been good stewards of God's creation. In particular, youth should learn the following key points:

- Repentance is not only a matter of confessing one's sins. It also is a matter of turning in a new direction, letting go of a bad habit, and adopting a good habit. The Greek word that we translate as *repent* means literally "to turn."

- The **Book of Jonah** is a story of repentance in which many elements of God's creation play key roles. This story emphasizes the importance of confessing and changing our ways as well as God's intense love for all of creation.

- We all have fallen short when it comes to caring for God's creation, and we all have opportunities to change our ways and take on practices that benefit the environment.

- Repentance is best done in the context of a Christian community, where brothers and sisters in Christ can support one another and hold one another accountable.

Getting Ready

As you prepare for this session, read the material on pages 56–59. If you have questions, additional resources are available at *burst.abingdonyouth.com*.

In the days leading up to this session, reflect on ways in which you have fallen short when it comes to being a steward of God's creation. Think about things that you carelessly throw away, energy that you waste by taking unnecessary car trips or leaving lights on, water that you waste by keeping the faucet running while you brush your teeth, or toxins that you release into the air or water supply by not properly disposing of paint or batteries. Pray about these things, confessing of your sins and asking for God's guidance as you take on greener, more healthful, and more faithful habits.

This session is not about making youth feel guilty for ways they may have hurt the environment. On the contrary, it is an opportunity to give over to God their past shortcomings and to commit to new ways of living. Be prepared to give examples of mistakes you've made with regard to the environment, what you've learned from these mistakes, and how you've changed.

✆ Food Ideas

Provide environmentally friendly snacks such as fresh, organic, locally grown fruits and vegetables. Consider also serving "shade grown" coffee: coffee that is grown within an ecosystem that doesn't require clearing trees or using chemical pesticides and fertilizers. (Look for one or more of the following certifications on the coffee packaging: "Certified Organic + Certified Shade," "Bird Friendly," or "USDA Organic.")

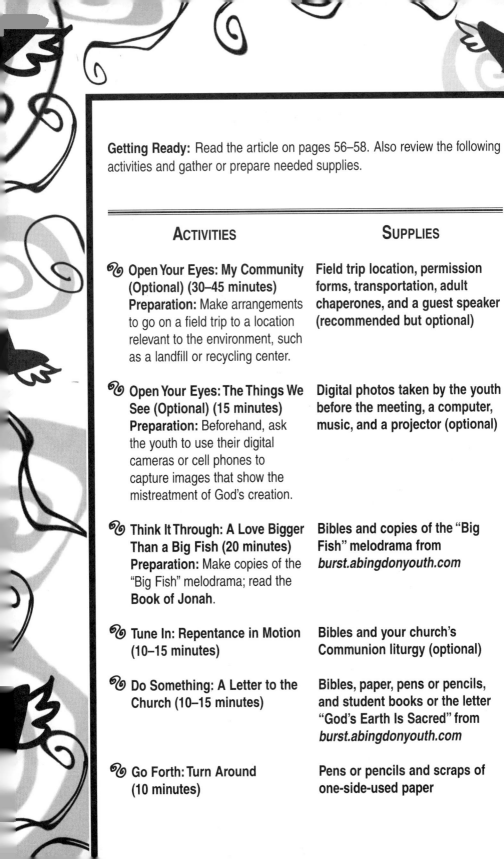

Getting Ready: Read the article on pages 56–58. Also review the following activities and gather or prepare needed supplies.

ACTIVITIES	SUPPLIES
Open Your Eyes: My Community (Optional) (30–45 minutes) **Preparation:** Make arrangements to go on a field trip to a location relevant to the environment, such as a landfill or recycling center.	Field trip location, permission forms, transportation, adult chaperones, and a guest speaker (recommended but optional)
Open Your Eyes: The Things We See (Optional) (15 minutes) **Preparation:** Beforehand, ask the youth to use their digital cameras or cell phones to capture images that show the mistreatment of God's creation.	Digital photos taken by the youth before the meeting, a computer, music, and a projector (optional)
Think It Through: A Love Bigger Than a Big Fish (20 minutes) **Preparation:** Make copies of the "Big Fish" melodrama; read the **Book of Jonah**.	Bibles and copies of the "Big Fish" melodrama from *burst.abingdonyouth.com*
Tune In: Repentance in Motion (10–15 minutes)	Bibles and your church's Communion liturgy (optional)
Do Something: A Letter to the Church (10–15 minutes)	Bibles, paper, pens or pencils, and student books or the letter "God's Earth Is Sacred" from *burst.abingdonyouth.com*
Go Forth: Turn Around (10 minutes)	Pens or pencils and scraps of one-side-used paper

Open Your Eyes: My Community (Optional)

This session will be strongest if the youth spend it on a field trip. Ideally, you should plan for the group to visit a city landfill, a waste-processing facility, a recycling center, a polluted stream, or some other location that illustrates the environmental realities in your community. Try to find a location where your group can visit for about 15–30 minutes. Give the youth permission forms, and recruit drivers as necessary.

You will need a field trip location, transportation, permission forms, and adult chaperones. A guest speaker is recommended but optional.

When planning your trip, think creatively about persons in your community who would make good "interpreters" of the setting. For example, a gardening expert or an entomologist could talk about invasive bug or plant species brought in through human activity that are doing great damage to local habitats or crops. (An alternative activity is below.)

When you have gathered the youth at the field trip location, review with them the details of the past four sessions. (You might also do this review in the car or bus as you travel to your location.) Ask questions such as:

Note: Field trip opportunities in your area might be limited during your usual meeting time, so consider moving your meeting time to correspond with the days and hours of operation of your chose site.

• What are some of the things that you have learned over the last four sessions about caring for creation?

• What actions have you taken to be a better steward of creation—either in response to this series or because of what you've learned elsewhere?

• Are there actions you've tried to take but couldn't or habits that you've tried to develop but haven't been able to? Why, do you think, has making these changes been so difficult?

• How might God be calling us, as a group, to care for creation?

If you have invited a speaker for this activity, introduce the him or her and tell the youth a little bit about his or her credentials and experience. Have the expert talk about how the work she or he does

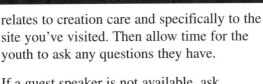

relates to creation care and specifically to the site you've visited. Then allow time for the youth to ask any questions they have.

Note: Take time during your opening activity to follow up on the goals the youth made for "The Three *Rs*" in the previous session (page 54).

If a guest speaker is not available, ask questions such as:

- How is this facility helping our environment? How is it hurting our environment?

- What has surprised you about this location? What have you learned that you didn't know before?

- How are we directly or indirectly responsible for the environmental problems or hazards we see in front of us?

- How does our visit to this site give you a different perspective on the things you use and throw away?

You may need to do some research on the site you visit in order to answer the teens' questions and to keep the discussion moving in a fruitful direction.

Before or after your discussion, allow the youth to observe the site. (Establish boundaries for safety purposes.) Then return to your meeting space, or continue with the rest of the session "on location."

Open Your Eyes: The Things We See (Optional)

If a field trip is not an option, do this activity instead.

Beforehand, ask the youth to use their digital cameras or cell phone cameras to collect during the week images of things regarding the state of God's creation that they think God would not approve of. Have the youth e-mail the photos to you or bring them on a flash drive or a memory stick that is compatible with the computer you'll be using.

You will need photos that the youth have taken during the week, a computer, music, a projector (optional).

Have the youth put all of their pictures in a common folder on the computer. (Alternatively, have all of the youth turn in their photos in advance, and ask one of the youth to put together a slide show or video set to an appropriate "green" song such as "Big Yellow Taxi," originally written and recorded by Joni Mitchell but recorded by several other artists as well.) Links to some songs that will work with this activity are available at *burst.abingdonyouth.com*.

Ask the youth to view the photos in silence as you scroll through them. Encourage the youth to not just look at the images but also to think about how God, the Creator, would respond to these images.

After the youth have viewed all of the images, toss an apple or an inflatable globe (or another object related to the subject of creation care) to one of the youth. Ask her or him to say which photo stood out most for her or him and to tell why. Then have that youth toss the apple or ball (or other object) to another youth. Continue until all have had an opportunity to talk.

Think It Through: A Love Bigger Than a Big Fish

Hand out copies of the "Big Fish" melodrama from *burst.abingdonyouth.com*. Ask youth to volunteer to play the roles of Jonah, God, the big fish, the ship captain, sailors, animals, and members of the chorus. Have the youth spontaneously act out the script as they read it.

> **You will need** Bibles and copies of the "Big Fish" melodrama from *burst.abingdon youth.com*.

After the melodrama, say: "This is a humorous take on a story that is filled with humor. Before we take a closer look at it, let's reread the last chapter of the **Book of Jonah**."

Ask volunteers to read aloud **Jonah 4.** Then ask the following questions to help clarify the story's details:

• What did God ask Jonah to do? (*preach a message of destruction to the city of Nineveh*)

• What happened when Jonah actually did what he was told to do? (*The people of Nineveh repented, so God spared them.*)

• Why was Jonah so angry with God? (*because God spared the wicked city of Nineveh*)

• What did God say God was concerned about? (*the people and creatures in Nineveh*)

Then ask:

• One of the things that sets apart the story of Jonah is the involvement of so many non-human creatures and other parts of God's creation. In addition to the famous big fish, a storm, a bush, a worm, the sun, and the wind are all involved in the lesson that Jonah learns. What, do you think, does this story tell us about God and about creation? (*God speaks to us through creation. God cares about all aspects of creation, not just human beings.*)

• This story involves several acts of repentance. Jonah in the belly of the fish repents of his arrogance. And the Ninevites repent of their sin against God and change their ways. Which of these acts of repentance, do you think, is more genuine? Why?

• Much as Jonah went to Nineveh to warn the Ninevites about their ways, many current-day prophets have been warning us about the harm we're doing to creation. Who are some of these prophets? (Especially lift up prophets in your congregation and community.)

• What can we learn about repentance from Jonah's story?

• When it comes to how you treat God's creation, of what do you need to repent?

Tune In: Repentance in Motion

Say: "In the **Book of Jonah,** all of the people of Nineveh repented together. In the Christian church, we have a tradition of corporate confession, meaning that we confess our sins in the presence of God and one another, knowing that we need the presence of our brothers and sisters in the body of Christ to help us change. The reality is that none of us is without sin and that we all fall short of living life as God desires."

> **You will need**
> Bibles and your church's Communion liturgy (optional).

Ask the youth to form a circle and to leave a small amount of space between each of them.

Repent

Say, "I'm going to read some statements about the ways we interact with creation. If a statement is true for you, take a step toward the center and then step back to rejoin the circle. Each time you step in, think of your movement as a symbolic act of confession and repentance. Please maintain silence so that this may be a time of prayer."

Read the following statements, pausing briefly after each one so that individuals may step in and out. Be sure to participate yourself.

• I have thrown away things that could have been reused by others.

• I have failed to recycle most of the trash I produce.

• I have wasted food at home, school, or at restaurants.

• I have left electronic or electric devices on when they were not in use.

• I have dumped chemicals down the drain, without giving a thought to how they could affect the community's water source.

• I have turned up the heat in my house, instead of wearing warmer clothes.

• I do not walk, ride my bike, or take the bus to school most weekdays.

• I have taken hot showers that were longer than necessary.

• I have left the water running while I brushed my teeth.

• I have never planted a tree.

• I have taken a drive in my car for no real purpose beyond simply going for a drive.

• I have not replaced the disposable batteries in my electronic devices with rechargeable ones.

• I do not regularly track and try to improve my gas mileage in the car I drive.

• I have not had regular conversations with my family members about the amount of earth's resources we use.

• I do not pay attention to where the products I buy come from.

• I have not prayed for the healing of God's creation, other than when I do so during youth group or worship.

Afterward ask:

• What sorts of things went through your mind during this activity? (For example: Did you think of excuses for why you do or don't do certain things? Did you think of way in which you could change?)

• Why was it helpful to perform this act of repentance as a community? Was it intimidating to step forward to acknowledge your faults? Was it comforting to know that you weren't alone?

Say: "Here's the good news: When we confess our sins and open our hearts and minds to change, God forgives and heals us and gives us a chance to begin anew. In the name of Christ, you are forgiven. In this circle are amazing resources and creativity and energy. We are called to use all that we are for the benefit of others and for creation, because God's love extends to all that is."

Read aloud **Acts 2:37-47** as an example of a Christian community repenting of its sins, claiming God's grace and forgiveness, and changing its ways. Consider concluding this activity by reading the prayer of confession from your denomination or congregation's communion liturgy. Such a prayer, from The United Methodist Church, is included on page 69.

Do Something: A Letter to the Church

Have the youth read the letter "God's Earth Is Sacred," at *burst.abingdonyouth.com*. (If possible, save paper by projecting the letter onto a wall or a projection screen. If you must print it out, have youth share copies so that you can use fewer sheets of paper.) Explain that this is a portion of a letter from the National Council of Churches—an organization that represents several Protestant and Orthodox faith traditions—to all persons about environmental realities.

> **You will need**
> Bibles, paper, pens or pencils, and copies of the letter "God's Earth Is Sacred" from *burst.abingdon youth.com*. A computer and projector are optional.

Have one or more of the youth read the letter aloud, while everyone else follows along.

Then divide the youth into groups of three or four. Instruct the groups to begin to draft a letter to the entire congregation about the group's hopes, fears, and concerns for the future of the environment. Encourage the groups to lift up some of the things they've learned as a part of this study and, whenever possible, explain how their hopes and concerns relate to Scripture. Publish the letters on your congregation's or youth ministry's website.

Go Forth: Turn Around

Have the youth spread out, and give each person a scrap of paper and a pen or pencil. Invite the youth to spend some time in silence, confessing the ways in which they have fallen short when it comes to caring for creation. Specifically, they might reflect on some of the items from "Repentance in Motion" (pages 65–67).

> **You will need**
> pens or pencils and scraps of paper that have already been used on one side.

Remind the youth that repentance is not just about confession but also about turning around and going in a new direction. Ask the youth to keep that in mind as they think of one bad habit that they can turn into a good habit. (For example, if they are bad about leaving on electronic and electric devices that they aren't using, they could commit to turning off the lights, television, stereo, videogame consoles, and anything else that continues to use energy even when no one is using it. They could also commit to making sure to unplug chargers for cell phones, handheld games, and laptops when they aren't charging.)

Tell the youth to write their commitment on the scrap of paper. Then have the youth pair up, and have the partners tell each other about their commitments. Challenge partners to hold each other accountable to these commitments in the coming weeks.

Give the youth plenty of time to work, then close in prayer, repenting for ways in which you have failed to care for creation and asking for guidance as you turn in a new direction.

68

Confessional Prayer

Merciful God,
we confess that we have not loved you with our whole heart.
We have failed to be an obedient church.
We have not done your will,
we have broken your law,
we have rebelled against your love,
we have not loved our neighbors,
and we have not heard the cry of the needy.
Forgive us, we pray.
Free us for joyful obedience,
through Jesus Christ our Lord. Amen.

From A Service of Word and Table I ©1972,1980,1985, 1989 The United Methodist Publishing House; and A Service of Word and Table II ©1972, 1980, 1985, 1989 The United Methodist Publishing House. Used by permission.

REJOICE

Rejoice in the Lord always;
again I will say, Rejoice.
—*Philippians 4:4*

Rejoice in the Lord Always

Look up *rejoice* in a Bible dictionary, and you'll most likely be directed to the entry on *joy*. Joy is an inward feeling; rejoicing is the outward, visual or audible expression that arises from that feeling. Many experiences bring joy: a great meal, good news, wise children (**Proverbs 10:1**), the day of harvest (**Exodus 23:16**), and much more.

More frequently, though, joy in the Bible is associated with theological reflections on who God is and what God has done. One rejoices in response to an experience of God's deliverance (**Psalm 21:1**), forgiveness and restoration (**Psalm 30:5; 51:8, 12**), or steadfast love (**Psalm 21:6-7; 31:7-8**), for example. God's action in the world, now and in the past, is cause for rejoicing.

For those who embrace creation and don't just ignore it or see it as a backdrop for human activity, God's creative expression in the natural world is, likewise, a great source of joy. Think back on some of your own moments of engagement with the earth and its creatures and plants. Perhaps you have climbed a tree over and over again. Maybe you have whooped with delight after diving into a cool lake. Probably you have been amazed by a bug you discovered while walking in the woods or by a beautiful animal or flower at a wildlife sanctuary or arboretum. Rejoicing is one of the common responses when to the sight of the Grand Canyon or the ocean for the first time, but it's just as possible to experience joy when driving past field after field of soybeans in rural Iowa.

Rejoicing—the outward expression of our inner emotional feeling about God's creation—is essential in today's world. Much of the news about the environment is not great; frequently, it's quite scary. People desperately need to hear good news about the earth. Rejoicing in God's creation in no way denies or ignores the very real problems all around us. Instead, rejoicing is a way of reminding ourselves and

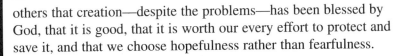

others that creation—despite the problems—has been blessed by God, that it is good, that it is worth our every effort to protect and save it, and that we choose hopefulness rather than fearfulness.

Unfortunately, joy is not the first response many young people have when they engage the natural world; fear is. Many of us are able to live in such a way that we rarely have to touch the unprocessed world of dirt and trees and freshly plucked berries. The result is that we forget where our food comes from—or for that matter, where everything comes from. (Hint: It's not from the store.) And since we have forgotten this, fear starts to creep into our lives. Whereas many little children find great joy upon discovering a caterpillar or huge spider web, by the time adolescence comes along, that joy has been replaced with a feeling that such things are gross or creepy.

There are two basic ways to replace fear with joy. First, we can rely on the power of memory. Reflecting upon past experiences of joy and delight in God's creation can put us at ease with the natural world. Second, we can enter more deeply into the natural world. Increase activity outdoors—particularly activity that includes consciously engaging with the world around us—to help us gradually shed our fear and experience joy.

In this final session, we rejoice together in God's creation. It's much easier to rejoice in creation when we're actually directly engaging with the natural world; so it is really important for you and the youth to be outside. You might meet at a nearby city or state park; or if a member of your church owns property that would give the youth an experience of the natural world, you might choose to meet there. Other options might include a local church or scout camp. You are strongly encouraged to plan a very positive experience of the natural world. Remember that rejoicing arises from actual experiences of joy, so please strive to leave the safety of your usual meeting space for the unpredictability of the natural world.

In addition to being a time of rejoicing in God's creative work expressed in creation, this session can also be a time for rejoicing in God's creative work within each of the youth. Over the course of this program, you have encouraged the youth to commit to new habits and ways of living. Invite them to talk about any changes they have made as a result of what they've learned and to tell how these changes have affected their lives, their relationships with God, and their relationships with the natural world. While these changes may be small, and while the youth have been practicing these new habits for only a few weeks, such actions are nonetheless cause for celebration and rejoicing. God is indeed still at work as the Creator of the world; and we, as persons created in God's image, are co-creators with God in bringing about a new creation. If ever there was a reason to rejoice, that surely is one.

In This Session

Youth should come away from this session rejoicing. In particular, youth should learn the following key points:

- While the problems facing the earth are very real and must be dealt with, there is still much about creation that is worthy of celebration. Rejoicing in the beauty of God's creation helps us better understand why God called creation "good" and better appreciate our role as caretakers of creation.

- We grow closer to God and God's creation when we spend time in the natural world. We all need to make time to enjoy God's handiwork.

- The Psalms are ancient Israel's hymns. Many of these hymns express how the ancient Israelites experienced God's love and power through God's creation.

- An important part of celebrating God's creation is reaffirming our role as caretakers. Caring for creation is not something that we do as individuals, but something that we do together as the body of Christ (**1 Corinthians 12:12-27**).

Getting Ready

As you prepare for this session, read the material on pages 70–73. If you have questions, additional resources are available at *burst.abingdonyouth.com.*

In the days leading up to this session, spend some time outdoors, enjoying God's creation. Visit a nearby city or state park and go for a hike; sit outside and look up at the stars on a clear evening; or ride a bicycle through the country. Whatever you decide to do, try to let go of any worries or concerns and be fully present in the natural world. Look for the beauty in the world around you, and offer a prayer of praise and thanksgiving to God the Creator.

This final session is an opportunity to rejoice and celebrate the wonders of God's creation, but it isn't just a big party. We should respond to the beauty of the world around us not only through songs of praise but also by reaffirming our role as caretakers. In this session, the youth will work together to come up with a plan for healing or protecting some aspect of creation.

✆ Food Ideas

Provide environmentally friendly snacks such as fresh, organic, locally grown fruits and vegetables. Consider also serving "shade grown" coffee: coffee that is grown within an ecosystem that doesn't require clearing trees or using chemical pesticides and fertilizers. (Look for one or more of the following certifications on the coffee packaging: "Certified Organic + Certified Shade," "Bird Friendly," or "USDA Organic.")

Getting Ready: Read the article on pages 70–72. Also review the following activities and gather or prepare needed supplies.

ACTIVITIES	SUPPLIES
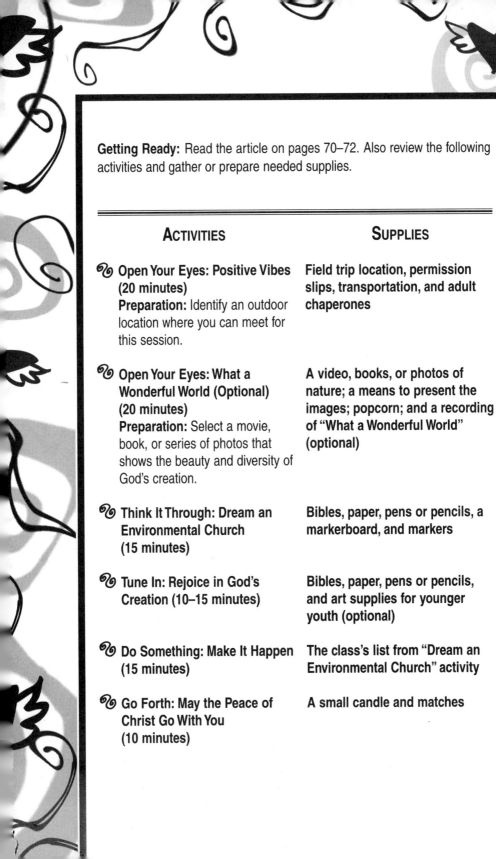 **Open Your Eyes: Positive Vibes (20 minutes)** **Preparation:** Identify an outdoor location where you can meet for this session.	Field trip location, permission slips, transportation, and adult chaperones
Open Your Eyes: What a Wonderful World (Optional) (20 minutes) **Preparation:** Select a movie, book, or series of photos that shows the beauty and diversity of God's creation.	A video, books, or photos of nature; a means to present the images; popcorn; and a recording of "What a Wonderful World" (optional)
Think It Through: Dream an Environmental Church (15 minutes)	Bibles, paper, pens or pencils, a markerboard, and markers
Tune In: Rejoice in God's Creation (10–15 minutes)	Bibles, paper, pens or pencils, and art supplies for younger youth (optional)
Do Something: Make It Happen (15 minutes)	The class's list from "Dream an Environmental Church" activity
Go Forth: May the Peace of Christ Go With You (10 minutes)	A small candle and matches

Open Your Eyes: Positive Vibes

For the reasons explained on page 71, try to hold this session outdoors in a location where the youth can experience the natural world. Locations might include a state or city park, a church or scout camp, or the property of a member of your church. You might choose to have your group go for a hike, canoe down a river, or observe wildlife in their natural habitat. The goal should be to give the youth a positive experience of nature.

> **You will need** a field trip location, transportation, permission slips, and adult chaperones.

As necessary, send out permission forms, enlist additional helpers, arrange for transportation, make reservations, and so on. If a trip is not possible, a simple picnic on the church grounds will work well too. Provide good, homemade food rather than pre-packaged snacks.

Gather the group at your outdoor location, and encourage the youth to be mindful of the environment around them. Then ask:

• What are your favorite things to do outside, in the natural world?

• When and how have you been afraid of the "wild"?

• When you think about the world around you, what gives you a reason to rejoice?

Open Your Eyes: What a Wonderful World (Optional)

If an outdoor session isn't possible, select a video or a series of photos that show the diversity and beauty of the world. Several suggested video titles are provided at *burst.abingdonyouth.com*. Project the movie or photos or as large a screen as possible. Provide popcorn, popped in the room so that the smell will fill the air.

> **You will need** a video, or photos of nature; a means to present the images; popcorn and popper; and a recording of "What a Wonderful World" (optional).

Allow the youth time to enjoy the images. If you use projected photos, play a version of the song "What a Wonderful World," recorded most famously by Louis Armstrong, as a soundtrack to the images.

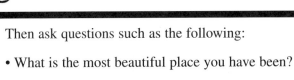

Then ask questions such as the following:

- What is the most beautiful place you have been?

- What were your favorite things to do outdoors when you were a child?

- What natural wonder would you most like to visit one day?

Think It Through: Dream an Environmental Church

Divide the youth into groups of 3 to 5. Hand out paper and pens or pencils.

> **You will need**
> Bibles, paper, pens or pencils, a markerboard, and markers.

Say: "During this series, we've learned a lot about the state of the natural world and about some of the things we can do to make things better. We all have gifts that we can use for the benefit of God's creation. But our strength as individuals is not nearly as great as our strength as a community."

Ask a youth to read aloud **1 Corinthians 12:12-27.**

Invite the groups to imagine what the church could be like if Christians were to take seriously our role as caretakers of creation in every part of church life—from building and property to worship to programs and ministries. Ask the youth to draw pictures of their vision of an environmental church, make lists of ways in which such a church cares for the environment, or create a sample church newsletter or website that illustrates ways in which such a church is committed to creation care.

Give the groups several minutes to work. If groups get stuck, help them out with suggestions such as, "How could we use less paper in worship or Sunday school?" "How could we as a church use less water?" "How could we encourage members of the church to make changes to their daily habits so that they benefit the environment?"

Then have each group present its ideas to the others. Use a marker to list these ideas on a markerboard. Rejoice at the vision being shared by affirming the groups' ideas with applause and words of praise.

After each group has presented its ideas, talk about what next steps they will need to take to make these dreams a reality. Listen carefully, take notes, and support the teens' ideas.

Tune In: Rejoice in God's Creation

Say: "One of the ways the ancient Israelites rejoiced and expressed their feelings about God's activity in creation was through the ancient hymns that we know as the Psalms."

> **You will need**
> Bibles, paper, pens or pencils.

Divide the youth into pairs or trios. Assign to each group one of the following psalms, with its accompanying question. (It's OK if some Scriptures are not used or are assigned to more than one group.)

- **Psalm 8:** What role do humans play within God's creation?

- **Psalm 29:** Why and how did the psalmist use the image of a thunderstorm to talk about God's relationship with creation?

- **Psalm 96:** Why is God worthy of being revered above all else?

- **Psalm 104:** What does this psalm say about the relationships between living things, particularly about the food chain.

Ask the groups to read their assigned psalm and to discuss the accompanying questions. Then challenge the groups to use their own words to write a psalm that rejoices in God's creation. The psalm may be as long or as short as they choose.

Do Something: Make It Happen

Return to the ideas for an environmental church that the youth came up with for the "Dream an Environmental Church" activity on pages 77–78. Work together to select one thing that your youth ministry can do to help your congregation better care for creation.

> **You will need**
> the list of ideas your group created for the activity "Dream an Environmental Church," above.

Divide the youth into three groups:

Group 1 should identify persons in the congregation and community who need to be involved for this effort to be successful.

Group 2 should determine what research needs to be done. (For example, if your class decides that the church needs to use less electricity, the group will need to identify how much electricity the

Burst: Green Church

church currently uses and set a reasonable goal for lowering the number of kilowatt-hours the church uses.)

Group 3 should focus on promotion. How will the class alert the church to the problem and the solution?

Give the groups a few minutes to work. Visit each group to offer help or suggestions. Then have each group present what it came up with. Based on the groups' suggestions, identify what tasks need to be undertaken in the coming weeks to make the plan a reality. Ask for volunteers to commit to these tasks. Identify leaders who can follow up and make sure that everything that needs to be done is being done.

Go Forth: May the Peace of Christ Go With You

Gather everyone into a circle. Light a small candle that can be passed easily from person to person, and hold it in your hands.

> **You will need** a small candle and matches.

Give the youth a moment to reflect on the parts of creation that bring them joy. Then pass around the candle. Instruct each youth that, when he or she has the candle, he or she is to name something about God's creation that he or she celebrates.

When the candle comes back to you, close with this Celtic blessing:

> May the peace of the Lord Christ go with you,
>   wherever he may send you,
> May he guide you through the wilderness,
>   protect you through the storm.
> May he bring you home rejoicing
>   at the wonders he has shown you,
> May he bring you home rejoicing
>   once again into our doors.
> In the name of the Father, the Son, and the Holy Spirit. Amen.

Organize a Church-Wide Green Study

A church-wide green study will give children, youth, and adults in your congregation an opportunity to explore together practical ways to respond to God's call to be good stewards. A church-wide program offers opportunities for learning, for intergenerational projects and activities, and for reaching out to the community through the programs and activities to address critical environmental concerns.

In addition to BURST: GREEN CHURCH, these resources are available for a church-wide green study:

Adults

- *Green Church: Reduce, Reuse, Recycle, Rejoice!* by Rebekah Simon-Peter

- *Leader Guide for Green Church: Reduce, Reuse, Recycle, Rejoice!* by Pamela Dilmore and Rebekah Simon-Peter

Children

- *Green Church: Caretakers of God's Creation*

All Ages

- *7 Simple Steps to Green Your Church,* by Rebekah Simon-Peter

Plans for a Church-Wide Green Study

Organize your study on a weeknight or during the Sunday school hour. If you choose a weeknight, begin with a meal (30 minutes), followed by an intergenerational gathering that features a green topic (15 minutes). This may include a presentation, skits, music, and an opening prayer. Then allot 60 minutes for age-specific classes.

If you do the study during Sunday school, begin with an intergenerational gathering that features a green topic. Then allot 30–40 minutes for age-specific classes.

Choose a schedule that works best for your congregation. End your program with a church-wide celebration of your green study. Consider including some of the following elements in your celebration: snacks (see page 7 for ideas), music, displays of projects that were completed as a part of the sessions, Scripture readings, prayers (possibly including some of those in this book, and information from some of the sources provided at *burst.abingdonyouth.com* and in the adult and children's materials.